Xenophon's Socrates

Other Titles of Interest from St. Augustine's Press

Gerhart Niemeyer, *Between Nothingness and Paradise*

Plato, *The Symposium of Plato: The Shelley Translation* (translated by Percy Bysshe Shelley)

Aristotle, *Aristotle – On Poetics* (translated by Seth Benardete and Michael Davis)

Michael Davis, *The Poetry of Philosophy: On Aristotle's* Poetics

Rémi Brague, *Eccentric Culture: A Theory of Western Civilization*

Roger Scruton, *An Intelligent Person's Guide to Modern Culture*

Roger Scruton, *On Hunting*

Roger Scruton, *The Meaning of Conservatism*

Josef Pieper, *Leisure, the Basis of Culture*

Josef Pieper, *Enthusiasm and Divine Madness: On the Platonic Dialogue* Phaedrus

Stanley Rosen, *Nihilism: A Philosophical Essay*

Stanley Rosen, *The Ancients and the Moderns: Rethinking Modernity*

Stanley Rosen, *Plato's Symposium*

Stanley Rosen, *Plato's Sophist: The Drama of Original and Image*

Stanley Rosen, *Plato's Statesman*

Seth Benardete, *Herodotean Inquiries*

Seth Benardete, *Achilles and Hector: The Homeric Hero*

Seth Benardete, *Sacred Transgressions: A Reading of Sophocles' Angigone*

Henrik Syse, *Natural Law, Religion, and Rights*

Jacques Maritain, *Natural Law: Reflections on Theory and Practice*

Ronna Burger, *The Phaedo: A Platonic Labyrinth*

Joseph Cropsey, *Polity and Economy: With Further Thoughts on the Principles of Adam Smith*

Ian S. Ross, ed., *On the Wealth of Nations: Contemporary Responses to Adam Smith*

G.A.J. Rogers, ed., *Leviathan: Contemporary Responses to the Political Theory of Thomas Hobbes*

Bosanquet, Bernard, *The Philosophical Theory of the State and Related Issues*

Leszek Kolakowski, *My Correct Views on Everything*

Xenophon's Socrates

Leo Strauss

Foreword by Christopher Bruell

ST. AUGUSTINE'S PRESS
South Bend, Indiana

Manufactured in the United States of America

2 3 4 5 6 26 25 24 23 22 21 20

Cataloging in Publication Data

Strauss, Leo.
    Xenophon's Socrates / by Leo Strauss
        p.   cm.
    Originally published: Ithaca, N.Y.: Cornell University Press,
    1972.
    Includes index.
    ISBN 1-890318-95-7 (cloth: alk. paper)
    1. Socrates. 2. Xenophon. Memorabilia. 3. Xenophon.
    Apology. 4. Xenophon. Symposium. 5. Philosophy, ancient.
    III. Title.
    B317. S78 1998
    183'.2—dc21   97-37673
                                                              CIP

Paperback edition ISBN: 1-58731-965-9

∞ The paper used in this publication meets the minimum requirements of
the American National Standard for Information Sciences—Permanence
of Paper for Printed Materials, ANSI Z39.4888–1984.

Editor's Note

With this volume Professor Strauss completes his study of the Socratic writings of Xenophon, begun in *Xenophon's Socratic Discourse: An Interpretation of the "Oeconomicus"* (Cornell University Press, 1970). Along with *On Tyranny* (Cornell University Press, 1968), these volumes constitute a monumental scholarly effort to restore the traditional dignity of Xenophon as a wise writer and to give a lesson in the ancient art of writing. They are almost indispensable guides to the charm, grace, and profundity of Xenophon and thereby teach much about the beliefs that have rendered him incomprehensible.

But of greater importance, this study is an attempt to recover the true Socrates and, with that, the character of political philosophy itself. It investigates the origins of political philosophy, its possibility and intention, against the non-philosophic background from which it emerged. Thus, it is a clarification of the phenomena of a lost natural world which has been obscured by later traditions. Professor Strauss's reflections on Aristophanes and Xenophon are his way of seeing again a Socrates who is hardly understood because he seems so well understood. As is always the case with Professor Strauss's books, this one is difficult of access; but to those who wish to understand the texts and the phenomena to which they refer, his works are a permanent possession.

ALLAN BLOOM
General Editor
Agora Paperback Editions

Toronto

Preface

With this volume I complete my interpretation of Xenophon's Socratic writings. I wrote and published first an interpretation of the *Oeconomicus* because that work is, it seems to me, the most revealing and at the same time the most misunderstood of Xenophon's Socratic writings. It is the most revealing because in its central chapter Socrates is directly contrasted with a perfect gentleman. In interpreting the other Socratic writings, I could not help repeating some points which I had been compelled to make in the earlier publication. The reader who notices the repetitions will, I trust, forgive the prolixity and note that I could without impropriety have been more prolix.

L.S.

St. John's College
Annapolis, Maryland

Contents

Foreword

The publication by St. Augustine's Press of paperback editions of Leo Strauss's last two books on Xenophon, the last two books which he published in his lifetime, presents to a new generation of students works that have already perplexed more than one generation of readers since their first appearance in the early 1970s. It was to be expected that they would make extreme demands on their readers' seriousness, as well as on their alertness and concentration, their patience and perseverance: all of Strauss's writings do that. But even readers already familiar with his work, or especially such readers, are often surprised, not to say disconcerted, at encountering a reserve or economy of expression remarkable even for him, together with a lightness of tone which, if not unprecedented in his earlier writing, appears to be more pervasive than hitherto. One is all the more surprised, therefore, to discover from a letter written in the last year of his life to a scholar whom he held in the highest regard that Strauss himself considered these books to be his best works: "I am glad that you received my two books on Xenophon's Socrates. They are not the last thing I have written, but I believe they are the best and part of it may be of interest to you. They develop at some length, if not eo nomine, what I indicated in *The City and Man* p. 61 regarding the difference between Socrates and The Bible."[1] Yet as this also suggests,

[1] Letter to Gershom Scholem of 11/17/72; cf. letter of 9/6/72 to the same correspondent. Leo Strauss, *Gesammelte Schriften*, vol. 3, ed. Heinrich and Wiebke Meier (Stuttgart/Weimar: J. B. Metzler 2001), pp. 764–65 and 762.

a consideration of what Strauss can have meant by the judgment of his books that he expressed to Scholem may facilitate our access to them—by casting some light on the puzzling features already noted, if not also in other ways.

Let us see, then, whether what the two books themselves reveal to us about their character and intention makes intelligible such a judgment. They treat between them the four Socratic writings of Xenophon. The second of the books, *Xenophon's Socrates*, which treats three of these writings including the longest, has no "Introduction" but only a very brief "Preface." (The "Preface" calls attention to the fact that Strauss has repeated in the book "some points" which he "had been compelled to make in the earlier publication." He excuses himself to "the reader who notices the repetitions": one can infer that Strauss addresses himself to such readers and alerts them in the "Preface" to the fact that the second book will confirm the first in some significant respect or respects. This is only fitting, since he had devoted the first book to that one of Xenophon's Socratic writings which seemed to him "the most revealing and at the same time the most misunderstood.") By failing to supply the second book with an "Introduction," Strauss brought it about that the "Introduction" to the first, *Xenophon's Socratic Discourse*, serves as introduction to the whole constituted by the two volumes taken together. But that "Introduction" is itself rather brief, and the task of announcing the theme of the books is assigned to only one of its eight paragraphs. (The seven others are devoted to showing why someone concerned with that theme might reasonably turn to Xenophon and to distinguishing his four Socratic writings from one another, by way of indicating the particular character and significance of the one that the first book is to treat.) This paragraph, with which indeed the book opens, reads as follows:

The Great Tradition of political philosophy was orig-
inated by Socrates.

Socrates is said to have disregarded the whole
of nature altogether in order to devote himself
entirely to the study of ethical things. His reason
seems to have been that while man is not necessarily in need of knowledge of the nature of all
things, he must of necessity be concerned with
how he should live individually and collectively.

The singularity of this paragraph as an introduction to a
work or works of Strauss can be properly gauged only by a
thorough comparison with the ways in which he introduced
each of his other books. For present purposes, however, it
may suffice to cast a glance at the "Introduction" to the volume which stands closest to the two Xenophon books in
spirit and theme, if not also in time. (It stands closest in time,
if one considers only books written originally as books and
excludes collections of essays.) The first paragraph of the
"Introduction" to *Socrates and Aristophanes* reads as follows:

Our Great Tradition includes political philosophy and
thus seems to vouch for its possibility and necessity.
According to the same tradition, political philosophy
was founded by Socrates.

In comparing these two first paragraphs, we are struck at
once by their similarity—and only thereafter by a profound
difference. In the introduction to the Xenophon volumes,
Strauss no longer seeks an extrinsic warrant (in tradition or
elsewhere) for the "possibility and necessity" of political
philosophy. Nor does he offer a justification for returning to
the origin of political philosophy, that is, to Socrates, as he
had done a bit further on in the earlier introduction:

The problem of Socrates as we have sketched it . . . can
only be preparatory to "the problem of Socrates" as

stated by Nietzsche: The question of what Socrates stood for inevitably becomes the question of the worth of what Socrates stood for. In other words, the return to the origins of the Great Tradition has become necessary because of the radical questioning of that tradition. . . .

The counterpart, in the Xenophon introduction, to those lines is a remark which Strauss makes almost in passing:

Our age boasts of being more open to everything human than any earlier age; it is surely blind to the greatness of Xenophon. Without intending it, one might make some discoveries about our age by reading and rereading Xenophon.

Here, in other words, it is not Socrates or political philosophy that is called before the bar (a bar belonging to, if not constituted by, "our age"); it is rather "our age" about which one could (from a perspective to be unfolded in the works before one) reach a fitting judgment, provided that one would still be concerned to do so. And by departing in this way from his practice of justifying his studies by appeals to concerns rooted in our particular situation, a practice that had still left its traces even on *Socrates and Aristophanes*, Strauss indicates that he has gone further in his books on Xenophon's Socrates than he had ever permitted himself to do before—for Strauss, too, "refused to separate from one another wisdom and moderation" (*Xenophon's Socrates* p. 78)—in presenting what he regards as the highest subject matter as it appears in (or to) itself.

But in describing these books as his best works, Strauss must have thought not merely of their subject matter and point of view but also of the manner of its treatment. What, then, is the necessary or appropriate manner for presenting, so far as possible, the philosophic life as it appears in and to itself? Since Strauss chose to tackle this task by way of a treatment of Xenophon's Socrates, we can assume that he regarded Xenophon and his Socrates as models also in this respect. After noting, therefore, that Xenophon has Socrates refer to certain "'physiological' questions"—that is, to questions belonging to the sphere of Socrates' "main concern" (*Xenophon's Socrates* p. 8)—at "an advanced stage of a drinking party where a greater *parrhesia* [outspokenness] is in order than elsewhere," Strauss comments: "The 'physiological' part of his [Socrates'] wisdom, nay, his whole wisdom can be shown without disguise only 'in fun'; so close is the connection between wisdom and laughter." (*Xenophon's Socrates* p. 170; cf. p. 92) Noting, on another occasion, that Xenophon has Socrates explain a remark of his only after an intelligent question or objection has been put to him, Strauss comments: "To state clearly what he means, he must apparently be sure that the one to whom he talks does some thinking." (*Xenophon's Socrates* p. 82; cf. p. 122) For our present purpose, this comment appears to create a greater difficulty than the preceding one: a writer, too, can express himself light-heartedly, not to say jocularly, but can he respond to his reader's questions or objections? Yes, if the same remark can mean one thing to someone who merely "takes it in" but quite another to one who, following the implicit argument on his own, puts to it at each stage the correct questions.

I will add two remarks which, at or about the time when he was writing these books, Strauss made to a young student of his acquaintance. Regarding *Xenophon's Socratic Discourse*, he said, while he was still working on it, that it is "the first book in which I address myself solely to an intelligent younger man *monos pros monon* [one alone to one alone]." Sometime after the completion of *Xenophon's Socrates*, he was asked by the student about its strange beginning and equally strange ending. (The beginning calls attention to the derivation from a verb that can mean "remembering one's grudge" of the term used for the title of the longest of the Socratic writings; the ending appears to go out of its way to associate Xenophon himself with a character of his who was a critic of Socrates.) Strauss replied: "As for Xenophon's possible critique of Socrates, it is ironical: he resented his corruption." It is safe to assume that what was true of Xenophon vis-à-vis Socrates was true also of Strauss: that he, too, "resented" his corruption at the hands of Socrates (and others) and therefore made such corruption *the* theme of his last two Xenophon books. (Compare *Xenophon's Socrates* p. 171 toward the bottom.)

As this suggests, to the right kind of reader Strauss presents in these books, as in no other books of his, also himself: himself as he truly was, *monos pros monon*. For that reader will be one who, awake to each remark of Strauss (who mentions something if he has noticed that it is important), continues to look in the direction pointed out to him until he has seen what Strauss, too, saw. And, seeing it (what Strauss saw, as he saw it), he draws close to, comes to know, not only the subject matter but also the make of the man who has helped to guide him toward it.

A Note on the Texts Treated in the Two Books

In seeking indication of the overall view of Xenophon's Socratic writings by which Strauss took his bearings in his treatment of each one of them, we must not lose sight of the singleness of purpose uniting his two books. As an additional example of their unity, we might mention the facts that the "Introduction" and therewith the first book altogether all but begins with a reference to the "powerful prejudice which emerged in the course of the nineteenth century and is today firmly established" according to which "Xenophon is so simple-minded and narrow-minded or philistine that he cannot have grasped the core or depth of Socrates' thought"; whereas the second book confides its last word to an "Appendix" which locates the "most telling" manifestation of such prejudice in a certain nineteenth century German scholar and goes on to indicate how the specific limitation of that scholar (which made him "blind to the greatness of Xenophon") would have looked from Xenophon's own point of view. It can no longer be surprising therefore that, while it is the "Introduction" that provides a synoptic account of the three texts treated in the second book, it is left to the "Preface" to supply a piece of information necessary to a full appreciation of the importance that Strauss attached to the single text which he treated in the first.

The longest of Xenophon's Socratic writings is the one whose title is usually rendered as Memorabilia (Recollections). As Strauss makes clear in the "Introduction," Xenophon (a man famous in his own right, who had "accomplished some deeds and pronounced some speeches which he considered worth remembering") devoted "his recollections par excellence" rather to what he remembered of his teacher, Socrates. More precisely, he devoted those recollections to establishing Socrates' justice, since the first or shorter part of the text in question is devoted to showing that Socrates was innocent of the charges on which he was convicted by an Athenian jury and put to death, while the second or longer part is devoted to showing how Socrates benefited his companions (and others). This means, according to Strauss, that the other three Socratic writings "are devoted to Socrates *tout court* or to Socrates even if he transcends justice." It is one of these that Strauss chose to treat in the first book. Which one and why? As he explains, the three texts which treat Socrates *tout court* divide the task among themselves. The *Symposium* is devoted to Socrates' deed or deeds; the *Apology of Socrates to the Jury* to his deliberating; and the *Oeconomicus*, the text chosen for treatment in the first book, to his speaking or conversing. According to the "Introduction," the reason would seem to be that the *Oeconomicus* is "Xenophon's Socratic *logos* or discourse par excellence." To this reason, the "Preface" adds that "in its central chapter Socrates is directly contrasted with a perfect gentleman" (that is, a man who embodies the virtues treated in Books III–V of Aristotle's *Nicomachean Ethics*, for example, or those about which Socrates was always inquiring according to *Memorabilia* I.1.16). The two reasons are linked. The contrast between Socrates and the perfect gentleman was of paramount interest to Socrates himself: it was to learn about a gentleman's virtue that Socrates sought one out. (*Oeconomicus* VI–VII and XI) And it was the conversation to which that initiative on his part led that was the "Socratic *logos* or discourse par excellence."

Two of Xenophon's Socratic writings, the *Symposium* and the *Apology of Socrates to the Jury*, have a namesake (or near namesake) among the Platonic dialogues. Xenophon's *Symposium*, too, presents Socrates at a dinner/drinking party. The host is not the poet Agathon but rather a wealthy Athenian gentleman by the name of Kallias; and eros is only one among a number of themes discussed. (Kallias is a Platonic character, as well: the host of the gathering portrayed in the *Protagoras* at which, curiously enough, almost all of the participants in Plato's *Symposium* are also present.) Xenophon's *Apology of Socrates*, unlike Plato's, gives only excerpts from the speeches made by Socrates at his trial; on the other hand, it presents the reasoning (deliberation) that led him to conduct his defense in the provocative manner in which he did. Socrates' trial is treated by Xenophon also in the *Memorabilia*. (I.1–2 and IV.8) There he presents, as Plato did not, a number of the remarks that had been made by Socrates' accusers. (I.2) Strauss's summary orientation implies—what his books also show—that despite these and other differences of presentation (see further *Xenophon's Socrates* pp. 53 and 83, for example, as well as *Xenophon's Socratic Discourse* p. 164) Xenophon's Socrates is identical to the Socrates of the Platonic dialogues.

CHRISTOPHER BRUELL

Suggestions for Further Reading

A. Translations of Xenophon's Socratic Writings

1. *Memorabilia*, translated and annotated by Amy L. Bonnette (Ithaca: Cornell University Press 1994).

2. *The Shorter Socratic Writings (Apology of Socrates to the Jury, Oeconomicus, and Symposium)*, edited by Robert C. Bartlett (Ithaca: Cornell University Press 1996).

B. Other Writings of Leo Strauss on Xenophon

1. "The Spirit of Sparta or the Taste of Xenophon," *Social Research* VI:4, pp. 502–36.

2. *On Tyranny*, edited by Victor Gourevitch and Michael S. Roth (Chicago: The University of Chicago Press 2000).

3. "The Origins of Political Science and the Problem of Socrates: Six Public Lectures," *Interpretation* XXIII:2, pp. 158–78.

4. "Greek Historians," *The Review of Metaphysics* XXI, pp. 656–66.

5. "Xenophon's *Anabasis*," *Studies in Platonic Political Philosophy* (Chicago: The University of Chicago Press 1983), pp. 105–36.

C. Discussions of Strauss's Works on Xenophon

1. "Philosophy and Politics I–II," by Victor Gourevitch, *The Review of Metaphysics* XXII, pp. 58–84 and 281–328.

2. "Strauss on Xenophon's Socrates," by Christopher Bruell, *The Political Science Reviewer*, XIV, pp. 263–318.

Memorabilia

The title *Apomnemoneumata* may be rendered provisionally by "Recollections." *Apomnemoneuein* (or derivatives) occurs only once within the *Memorabilia* (I.2.31); there it means "resenting," "remembering one's grudge." To use this passage for the interpretation of the title is to begin with the height of absurdity, and we all are beginners. The title is misleading for a more obvious reason: it is silent on the fact that the book consists exclusively of recollections about Socrates. The title would be appropriate if we could assume that the most memorable experience that Xenophon ever had was his intercourse with Socrates and not, for instance, with Cyrus or with Agesilaos. We do make that assumption and expect to transform it into a certainty.

The *Memorabilia* opens as follows: "Many times I wondered by what possible speeches those who indicted Socrates persuaded the Athenians that he deserved death from the city. For the charge against him ran about as follows: Socrates commits an unjust act by not worshipping (respecting, believing in) the gods whom the city worships but carrying in other, novel divine things (*daimonia*); he also commits an unjust act by corrupting the young." Xenophon indicates that his quotation of the indictment is not quite literal. In this he proceeds like the Platonic Socrates (*Apology of Socrates* 24b8–c1). But while the changes made by the Platonic Socrates are very considerable, the change made by Xenophon is almost negligible: he replaces the "leading in" of the original by "carrying in" (cf.

Plato, *Republic* 514b8). This difference can be taken as representative of the difference between Plato's presentation of Socrates and Xenophon's.

The Refutation of the Indictment

I.1. Since the indictment speaks of two crimes of Socrates, the refutation of the indictment consists of two parts, the refutation of the impiety charge and the refutation of the corruption charge. At the beginning of the refutation of the impiety charge Xenophon reminds us of the fact that Socrates was charged with not worshipping (believing in) the gods of the city. To refute that charge, Xenophon speaks of Socrates' sacrificing and his using divination; he devotes to sacrificing about 2 lines and to his using divination about 57 lines. The reason for this unequal treatment is this: while in regard to sacrificing Socrates behaved in an altogether normal or inconspicuous manner, in regard to divination he was notorious for saying that the *daimonion* gave him signs; this was probably the reason why he was accused of bringing in new *daimonia*. Yet Socrates was not guilty of any innovation, for the others who divine, say, from sacrifices, mean that the gods dissuade or persuade them through the sacrifices but say misleadingly that the sacrifices do this. Socrates however said exactly what he thought; he said that the *daimonion* gave him signs. In other words, Socrates' appeal to his *daimonion* is one kind of divination not different in the most important respect from the other generally known kinds. Yet Xenophon does not suggest that Socrates used the vulgar kinds of divination. Socrates' *daimonion* was very reliable. He told many of his companions to do this or not to do that on the ground that the *daimonion* foretold the outcome, and the outcome proved him right. Socrates would never have foretold the future to those of his companions to whom he did foretell it, if he had not trusted that he was foretelling the truth; but to whom can one trust in these matters except to a god? And if he trusted gods, how could he believe that there are no gods? Yet this argument hardly proves that Socrates believed in the existence of the gods of the city, and he had not been accused of atheism in the indictment. Yet Socrates went further. He did not merely make use in his way of divination, i.e., of his *daimonion*. He sent his "friends" (*epitēdeioi*) away to consult oracles about the proper subjects. Are the "friends" different from the "companions" (*synontes*) to whom he gave the benefit of his *daimonion?* When talking to these "friends" he did not speak of his *daimonion.* Or are they identical with the companions? Did he send his companions to the oracles when only approval of an intended course of action by a public oracle could protect them against the possibly harsh disapproval on the part of the city (cf. *Anabasis* III.1.5)? Or did he send them to an oracle when his *daimonion* remained silent? While Xenophon does not clear up this point, he makes quite clear what the proper questions to address to oracles are. The gods have given to men to know "the necessary things" or to learn all the arts and skills which are meant to lead them to their obtaining the various goods. What the gods reserved for themselves to know is precisely the most important thing in these matters, namely, the outcome of men's efforts: a man possessing the strategic art cannot know whether the exercise of that art will benefit him. Regarding the most important things in these matters one must consult the oracles, i.e., one must try to find out what is beneficial from the gods through divination, for the gods give signs to those to whom they are gracious. Regarding their most important matters Socrates sent his friends to consult the oracles: he did not consult the oracles for his own guidance;

as for his most important matters he relied on his *daimonion* alone, which he did not have to consult (cf. IV.3.12). Both those who deny that there is anything demonic (*daimonion*) in matters of this kind and those who consult oracles about things which men can know through their own god-given powers, are possessed (*daimonān*) and do what is gravely improper.

The previous argument is not quite sufficient, as Xenophon indicates at the beginning of the next part—the second or central part—of what he says in reply to the impiety charge. The previous argument is based on what Socrates did both at home and in public and what he said more or less in private. He may have conducted himself rather normally in deed and in speech —but what about his private thoughts? Xenophon now disposes of all possible suspicions by suggesting that Socrates was always in the open and always talking to large crowds: no hiding place was left for any private thoughts of his. More precisely, he says that Socrates was the whole day in the open in places where he could be together with as many people as possible and that he was talking most of the time, and everyone who wished could listen. And no one has ever seen him do, or heard him say anything impious or unholy. For he did not, in the manner of most of the others, converse about the nature of all things: he did converse about the nature of all things but in a manner different from that of most others. Those others consider the state of what the sophists call *kosmos* and the necessities that account for the various heavenly happenings (motions of stars, lightning, thunder, etc.). He thought that worrying about such matters is foolish for these three reasons. (1) Had these men given sufficient thought to the human things before they turned to the divine things (*daimonia*) or did they simply disregard the human things? ("Demonic" means here almost the same as what is called "natural" by others; perhaps Socrates' *daimonion* was in an outstanding manner something natural.) (2) Did they not see that man cannot find out those super-human things? For it is obvious that the men who think most highly of speaking on such matters behave like madmen. For the madnesses are opposite extremes surrounding a sane and sober or normal mean. For instance, some madmen fear nothing, while others fear everything; some madmen are not ashamed to say or do anything even in a crowd, while others believe that one should not even go out among men; some madmen reverence nothing while others reverence almost anything. Or, to use a previously given example, some believe that oracles will answer any question while others believe that they answer no question. Now as for those who worry about the nature of all things, some of them believe that being is only one and others believe that there are infinitely many beings; some believe that all things are always in motion and others believe that nothing is ever in motion; some believe that all things come into being and perish, others believe that nothing ever comes into being or perishes. This would seem to imply that according to the sane Socrates the beings are numerable or surveyable; those beings are unchangeable while the other things change, and those beings do not come into being or perish while the other things come into being and perish. It seems to imply, in other words, that there is a Socratic cosmology: Socrates did worry about the nature of all things and to that extent he too was mad; but his madness was at the same time sobriety: he did not separate wisdom from moderation (III.9.4). But all this is only implied. This example illustrates the general character of Xenophon's presentation of Socrates: he speaks almost exclusively of Socrates' normality; he only intimates his deviations from the normal. (3) Do the men who investigate the divine things (*theia*) hold that after they have acquired knowledge of the necessities by which the various. things come into being, they will be able to make those things, for instance, wind and rain, or are they fully satisfied with the mere knowledge of the necessities in question?—As for Socrates, he always conversed about the human things, considering what is pious, what is impious, what is noble, what is base, what is just, what is unjust, what is moderation, what is madness, what is courage, what is cowardice, what is a city, what is a political man, what is rule over human beings, what is a being fit to rule human beings, and the other things knowledge of which makes one a perfect gentleman while men ignorant of them deserve to be called slavish. (We note that in the enumeration of Socratic themes moderation—*sophrosyne*—and its opposite madness occupy the center.)

If Socrates conversed "always" about the human things by raising the "what is" questions regarding them, it is hard to see when he conversed about the nature of all things in his manner. It is also hard to see why Xenophon so rarely presents Socrates engaged in raising "what is" questions regarding the human things: at most 3 chapters out of the 49 chapters of the *Memorabilia* present Socrates engaged in this pursuit. Here again we see Xenophon pointing to something of the greatest importance but not, or hardly, presenting it. The typical Socratic conversation as presented by Xenophon is greatly misleading in regard to Socrates' main concern. That typical conversation stands in the same relation to his conversations about the "what is" of the human things, as those "what is" questions stand to his cosmology.

It follows that despite Socrates' always being in the open and talking most of the time to as many people as possible, what he thought was not manifest to his judges or to all. In addition, he was not always in the open; to say nothing of the nights and his sacrificing at home, he sometimes conversed in private (cf. III.10–11) and even with a single man (IV.2.8). Above all, even when he talked in public, he frequently raised questions instead of answering them, so much so that he was notorious for this practice (I.2.36, IV.4.9). Xenophon disposes of all these difficulties in the third or final part of his refutation of the impiety charge. He admits now that the points which he had made hitherto were not known to all Athenians. He now refutes the impiety charge by referring to a single fact known to all: Socrates' refusal to perjure himself by giving in to the clamor of the people when he presided in the Assembly of the people at the time of the trial of the generals who were in command at Arginusai. This strongest proof of Socrates' piety is however of dubious value since Socrates' exemplary conduct on that occasion could as well be regarded as proving his justice rather than his piety (IV.4.1–4; *Hellenica* I.7.15). Differently stated, "what all know" is precisely not what is going on in the mind of the doer (cf. *Anabasis* II.6.28; *Cyropaedia* VI.2.2) and therefore something which permits of a variety of interpretations; it is what he does or says but not what he silently deliberates. Xenophon continues as follows: Socrates' belief "in the gods' concern for man differed from the belief of the many, for the many believe that the gods know some things and do not know others. Socrates however held that the gods know everything, what is said, what is done, and what is silently deliberated, that they are everywhere present, and give signs to the human beings regarding all human things." When Xenophon spoke of what Socrates said to his "friends," he asserted that Socrates said that the gods give signs (only) to those to whom they are gracious (I.1.9). Socrates' belief that the gods know what is going on in the minds or hearts of men is meant to explain why he kept his oath. We may note that the belief of the many regarding the gods' knowledge is the mean between the extreme view held by Socrates according to which the gods know everything and the opposite extreme according to which they know nothing of the human things.

We are not surprised to see Xenophon finally stating that "the Athenians" were persuaded that Socrates was not sound (*sophron*) regarding the gods whereas, as he says immediately after, only "some" were persuaded that he corrupted the young. All the more remarkable is the fact that the refutation of the impiety charge occupies only about a third of the space occupied by the refutation of the corruption charge.

I.₂. The corruption charge meant that Socrates corrupted the young by his teaching. Therefore the answer to the question as to whether Socrates was a teacher and what, if anything, was the subject of his teaching, is a most important ingredient of the refutation of the corruption charge. Nothing had been said about Socrates' "teaching" or Socrates as a "teacher" in the refutation of the impiety charge: the impiety charge ultimately concerned what Socrates thought as distinguished from what he said.

The refutation of the corruption charge consists of two parts: a general refutation and the refutation of specific charges made by the accuser.

The general refutation is to the effect that a man like Socrates, who in addition to being pious was of the greatest continence and endurance, could not possibly corrupt anyone. On the contrary, he liberated many from impiety, lawlessness, incontinence, and sloth by inducing them to desire virtue and by giving them hope that they would become gentlemen if they took care of themselves. Yet he never claimed to be a teacher of virtue or gentlemanship, but by manifestly being virtuous or gentlemanly he made those who were spending their time with him hope that by imitating him they would become like him in this respect. Did he then think that virtue is not teachable? (Cf. Isocrates, *Against the Sophists* 17–18). Nor did he induce his companions to neglect their bodies nor did he make them lovers of wealth. Here again his example was decisive. He himself did not neglect his body, for he did not wish his care for his soul to be impeded by his body, nor did he take pay for associating with his companions, for he was concerned with his freedom. Those who take pay for their society are compelled to converse with those from whom they take pay. Socrates did not, and did not wish to, converse with everyone who wished to converse with him (cf. I.6.5). This does not necessarily contradict the fact that everyone who wished could listen to what Socrates said in public (I.1.10).

The first specific charge made by the accuser which is quoted by Xenophon contended that Socrates made his companions look down with contempt on the established laws and even on the established regime by saying that it is foolish to appoint the rulers of the city by lot; Socrates thus incited the young to violence. Xenophon does not even attempt to defend Socrates against the charge that he made subversive speeches to his companions; he only tries to show that men like Socrates do not favor violence and do not make others violent. Neither Socrates, because he was prudent (*phronimos*), nor his companions, who were under his influence, relied on violence for they regarded themselves as capable of "teaching" their fellow citizens what is advantageous or of persuading them in such matters. While Socrates made subversive speeches, he did not engage in subversive deeds.

Xenophon pursues the theme of Socrates' teaching further when he takes up the second charge brought forth by the accuser, the charge that made Socrates responsible for the many misdeeds committed by Kritias and Alkibiades, his associates; Kritias was the most violent man under the oligarchy and Alkibiades the most insolent man (*hybristotatos*) under the democracy. According to Xenophon these two men associated with Socrates in their youth because they held that by doing so they would become most able to speak and to act, i.e., to do the political things; they were attracted, not of course by Socrates' very great continence or moderation but because Socrates could with his speeches manage all his interlocutors in any manner he wished. Their temporary adhesion to Socrates presupposed therefore that Socrates "taught the political things," as Xenophon admits that he did in a reply to a possible objection. The political things are at the very least a part of the human things which Socrates always considered in his manner, for one cannot study the political things without sooner or later being compelled to raise the questions "What is a city?" and "What is a political man?" Moreover, as Xenophon admits in the same reply, Socrates taught moderation as a necessary preparation for the study of the political things (cf. IV.3.1). Moderation, whose opposite is *hybris,* is not the same as continence, whose opposite is incontinence. Socrates "taught" his young associates moderation, presumably because he handled in speech all his interlocutors in any manner he wished. Above all, he taught moderation by revealing himself to his companions as a perfect gentleman and by conversing in the most noble manner about virtue and the other human things. Xenophon does not say that Socrates' teaching of the political things was identical with his noble conversations about virtue. In a reply to another possible objection Xenophon takes issue with many of those who claim to philosophize and who assert that nothing ever truly learned, and in particular moderation, can ever be forgotten; this is the only philosophic discussion engaged in by Xenophon in his own name that occurs in his Socratic writings. He indicates clearly that moderation is acquired by practice rather than by learning, for the speeches teaching moderation, or the chastising speeches, become ineffective when the original experiences that give rise to the desire for moderation are forgotten by not being constantly acted upon.

Xenophon asserts that Kritias and Alkibiades became corrupted only after they had left Socrates and that Socrates was therefore in no way responsible for their misdeeds. He gives this example. Socrates rebuked Kritias for his low sexual desires in very strong terms partly in his presence and partly in his absence. As a consequence Kritias hated him and later, when he had become a legislator, he showed his resentment by laying down a law forbidding the teaching of the art of speeches. He justified that law by appealing to the popular prejudice against all philosophers. Xenophon asserts emphatically that the prejudice was wholly unfounded in the case of Socrates but he does not make clear the purport of that prejudice: were the philosophers hated as atheists or as men who make the weaker argument the stronger or on both grounds? He certainly does not deny that Socrates taught the art of speeches. One must wonder how the teaching of that art is related to the teaching of the political things, i.e., of speaking and of acting. Speaking seems to occupy the first rank: the man who is able to persuade, as distinguished from the man who dares to use violence, does not need any ally (I.2.11). Socrates as the unrivalled master of persuasion would then seem to be a man more fit to rule than anyone else. It is true, the art of speaking is not sufficient for making a man fit to rule; one must also be very continent (II.1) but Socrates fulfilled this condition to an extraordinary degree. Yet even more is needed: Socrates could do what he liked in speech with any interlocutor; could he do it in deed? Xenophon answers this question in the last part of his account of Socrates' relation with Kritias: Socrates did not question Kritias' right to lay down the prohibition against the teaching of the art of speaking; he even declared his willingness to obey Kritias' laws. He blamed indeed Kritias' sanguinary rule, but only in Kritias' absence, behind his back. The art of speaking requires as its indispensable supplement the ability to do and in particular to coerce (cf. *Anabasis* II.6.16–20). The question of the relation of speech and deed is akin to the question of whether continence or moderation is acquired by teaching or by practice.

Socrates' association with Kritias as presented by Xenophon differs strikingly from his association with Alkibiades as presented by Xenophon; the difference is slightly concealed by the fact that in his general appraisal of the two men he blames both of them equally. He gives no example of Socrates' rebuking Alkibiades, to say nothing of a conflict between Socrates and Alkibiades. (It is only fair to say that Kritias is less harsh on Socrates than Kritias' fellow legislator Charikles.) Instead, after having said that Kritias and Alkibiades, while still being together with Socrates, tried to converse with the most prominent political men, he gives a hearsay report of a conversation of the very young Alkibiades with his guardian, Perikles. This is the only conversation transmitted through the *Memorabilia* in which Socrates does not participate. Alkibiades asked the great man, "What is law?" on the ground that a man cannot be law-abiding if he does not know what law is. Xenophon prepares his reader for the discussion of "what is law" by his account of Socrates' conversation with the legislators Kritias and Charikles. Alkibiades refuted Perikles easily in the Socratic manner. Perikles had given an answer which is true only of laws enacted in a democracy. The refutation makes clear that what law is depends on the regime and then that a command of the ruler is law only if it is enacted after the ruled have been persuaded of its goodness. Not only is the refutation or the answer Socratic; the very question is Socratic. The young Alkibiades was a Socratic. It is true that the question which he raised is not mentioned among the "what is" questions which Socrates always considered; nor is it ever raised by the Xenophontic Socrates. This is another example of the limitation that Xenophon imposed on himself when writing his "recollections."

Xenophon opposes to Kritias and Alkibiades the true associates of Socrates—he mentions seven of them by name—who were together with Socrates not in order to become political or forensic orators but in order to become perfect gentlemen and then to make a noble use of household, servants, relatives, friends, the city, and fellow citizens. The true associates of Socrates were men who minded their own business (II.9.1) or led a strictly private life. But how could Socrates tolerate Kritias and Alkibiades in his company—men who sought his company only in order to become most able politicians, who were from the beginning eager for the political life, who were by nature the most ambitious Athenians? He probably hoped that through his influence they would become moderate also in their political activity. At any rate Socrates, who taught the political things, had two kinds of associates:

those desiring a most noble private life and those desiring a political career.

The third charge made by the accuser concerned Socrates' subverting paternal authority: he persuaded his companions that he would make them wiser than their fathers; he used the fact that the son may lawfully hold in bondage his father convicted of insanity as a proof that the wiser man may lawfully hold in bondage the more ignorant man. In his reply Xenophon speaks at some length of the distinction that Socrates drew between insanity and ignorance, but he does not deny that Socrates persuaded his companions that he would make them wiser than their fathers. The fourth charge by the accuser was to the effect that Socrates disparaged also the other kinsmen and the friends as inferior to the wise man since all good will is useless if one is not able to help; thus he led the young to think that he himself was most wise and most able to make others wise. Xenophon admits that Socrates said these things. He even said more. He said that everyone not only disparages but even removes what is useless in his body, although he loves his body more than anything else, surely more than anybody else's body. (We may remember that what is most important regarding generalship is whether being a general is beneficent to oneself—I.1.8). But all this does not mean more, according to Socrates, than that if one wishes to be helped or honored by others, one must help them and this requires that one must make every effort to become as sensible as possible.

The last charge made by the accuser concerned Socrates' alleged vicious use of the most vicious passages occurring in the works of the most celebrated poets; he mentioned one verse from Hesiod and nine verses from Homer; the verses from Homer were quoted by Socrates "many times." Xenophon knows that Socrates did not make a vicious use of those verses but he does not explain why he quoted the Homeric verses "many times"; in the immediate sequel of the verses in question Homer says that "not good is the rule of many, one should be ruler, one should be king." The accuser had traced Socrates' quoting the Homeric verses to his hostility to the common people. Xenophon rejoins that Socrates, himself a man of the people, was populist and a lover of human beings, as is shown by his never having taken fees for his being together with the many who longed for his company or with anyone who wished.

Xenophon draws the final conclusion that Socrates deserved not death but great honor from the city. That he did not deserve death appears if one considers his actions from the point of view of the laws. Xenophon enumerates six kinds of actions, punishable by death, from which Socrates abstained more than anyone else and of none of which he was even accused. Does he mean to say that not worshipping the gods and corrupting the young are not forbidden by law? He then observes that Socrates never caused the loss of a war, an armed rising, treason, or any other evil to the city: is treason not forbidden by law (cf. *Apol. Socr.* 25)? Xenophon's remark seems to show how necessary it is to raise the question "What is law?"

Socrates as Benefactor of His Companions

I.3. After having shown that the indictment of Socrates was entirely baseless, Xenophon turns to narrating how Socrates, far from harming anyone, even helped his companions, partly by showing by deed what kind of man he himself was and partly by conversing. He thus indicates the subject of the rest of the *Memorabilia*, i.e., of the bulk of the work. The plan of that part can be discerned to some extent by a summary comparison of its content with the subjects suggested by some distinctions, occurring in the work, of what we may call the objects of man's duties: the man himself, relatives, friends, and the men longing for political honor (I.2.48, II.1.19, III.6.2, 7.9, IV.4.17, 5.10). Those headings may refer to Socrates' conduct or to the conduct which he recommended to others or to both. By comparing the division referred to with the *Memorabilia* itself, one will observe that the subject "servants" (i.e., slaves) is omitted in that work, whereas it is treated at great length in the *Oeconomicus*.

The Man Himself

Xenophon follows first the "plan" of the indictment or of his refutation of the indictment by speaking of Socrates' piety and then of his continence. He even preserves to some extent the proportions of the preceding discussion by devoting almost twice as many lines to "continence" as to "piety."

In refuting the charge of impiety Xenophon had spoken very briefly of Socrates' sacrificing and then at considerable length of his use of divination as well as of his abstention from the study of nature. He now speaks rather extensively of his sacrificing, inserting in his speech on this subject a statement on Socrates' prayer, and much more briefly than in the first statement on his use of divination. Regarding sacrifices, the worship of ancestors, and the like, Socrates' speech and deed complied with the response of the Pythia who enjoins that one comply with the law of the city. Therefore there can be no more doubt that Socrates worshipped the gods of the city, although it still remains uncertain whether he believed in their existence. By bringing small sacrifices from his small means he did not think that he was worse off than those who bring frequent and large sacrifices from their many and large possessions; his authority for this thought is not the Pythia but

Hesiod. His reason for this thought is that otherwise wealthy knaves would be more pleasing to the gods than poor and honest men, and this would not be becoming for the gods while it would make men's lives not worth living. He deferred to no authority regarding his practice of praying. He prayed to the gods simply that they give him the good things, the gods knowing best what kind of things are good. This Xenophontic report reminds one in a general way of the *Second Alcibiades*. But there Socrates' final advice to Alkibiades is to this effect: since Alkibiades suffers from a specific unreasonableness (*megalopsychia*), he is not able to pray properly; therefore he should not pray and sacrifice at all for the time being. There is no suggestion in the *Second Alcibiades* that one should pray simply for the good things since the gods know best what kind of things are good. Be this as it may, the fact that the statement on Socrates' prayer is inserted into a report on Socrates' sacrificing makes one wonder about the relation of prayers and sacrificing: do the gods listen to prayers, reasonable or unreasonable, only if one has sacrificed to them according to one's means? Regarding divination Xenophon speaks now exclusively of Socrates' always following the signs or counsels given by the gods; he is now silent on the *daimonion*. As if to draw our attention to this silence, he uses the word *daimonion* in a different sense almost immediately after he has concluded his statement on Socrates' piety, i.e., near the beginning of his statement on Socrates' continence: Socrates' mode of life would be very helpful to everyone, unless something demonic intervened; was Socrates warned of imminent interventions of this kind by his *daimonion*? Giving a jocular interpretation of a Homeric story, Socrates traced Odysseus' not being transformed into a pig to both his continence and Hermes' prompting: Odysseus' continence and his being guided by Hermes foreshadow Socrates' continence and his being guided by his *daimonion*.

More than half of the statement on continence is devoted to continence in matters of sex. Xenophon reports a conversation between Socrates and himself which was occasioned by Socrates' having heard that Kritoboulos had kissed a handsome boy; Kritoboulos was present at the conversation; Xenophon defended Kritoboulos' action, which Socrates blamed severely as extremely foolhardy; Socrates apostrophized Xenophon by "you wretch" and "you fool." This is the only conversation with Xenophon that occurs in Xenophon's Socratic writings; Kritoboulos, who had occasioned the conversation and for whose benefit it was chiefly intended, occurs again as the interlocutor in one of the longest conversations presented in the *Memorabilia*, as the interlocutor in the *Oeconomicus*, and as an important character in the *Symposium*; Xenophon is insignificant compared with him. Furthermore, Xenophon is the only character in his writings who is ever apostrophized by his gentle and urbane master by "you wretch," "you fool," or anything like this. The apostrophe "you wretch" occurs only once more in the Socratic writings; in a story told by Socrates, Virtue herself calls Vice herself "you wretch." It is easy to see how Socrates could correspond to Virtue, but how could Xenophon correspond to Vice? "Unless indeed the care bestowed upon virtue is corruption" (I.2.8). It is easy for us to think that the light-hearted Xenophon rebuked by Socrates is the very young Xenophon who had not yet undergone the full weight of the complete Socratic training, whereas the virtuous Xenophon, presented in the *Anabasis*, is the finished product. Yet Xenophon is not the only interlocutor of Xenophon's Socrates who is in the early stages of his training and only he is given those unenviable epithets. One may therefore be prepared to consider that the unique conversation is not quite serious: Xenophon's Socrates, who is so unlike Aristophanes' Socrates since he does not study nature in the manner of the Aristophanean Socrates or of "most others," obviously imitates the Aristophanean Socrates who calls Strepsiades "you fool" or "you wretch" (*Clouds* 398, 68); does Xenophon imitate Strepsiades or perhaps the horseman Pheidippides?

I.4. Xenophon still follows the plan of the indictment by devoting this chapter to piety and the next one to continence.

At the beginning he refers to some written and oral criticisms of Socrates according to which Socrates has been most excellent in urging on or exhorting human beings to virtue but insufficient in leading them on toward it. Leading men on toward virtue is obviously more than urging them on. But it is less than teaching them virtue or making them virtuous. Xenophon does not deny that Socrates made his companions wise or wiser (I.2.52–53); he even asserts that he made them moderate (IV.3.2) or more pious, more moderate (IV.3.18) and more just (IV.4 end) at least partly by speeches. Xenophon proposes that those who are impressed by such criticism should consider not only what Socrates said in refuting those who believe to know everything but also what he passed his day with in saying to those who lived constantly with him; only by considering Socrates' speeches which were not merely protreptic or elenctic can one judge fairly whether he was able to improve his companions, to lead them to or into virtue. Xenophon here leaves the judgment to the reader: the reader must see for himself whether or not Socrates made his present interlocutor pious. That Xenophon makes these suggestions immediately after he has reported Socrates' first conversation on continence and before he reports his first conversation on piety is hardly an accident: continence is acquired by one's practice rather than by one's being convinced or persuaded of the goodness of continence, whereas in the case of piety, the core of which is belief in the gods, the convincing or persuasive speeches play a much greater, if not decisive, role.

Socrates had the conversation about piety or, to be more precise, about the divine—for it is thus that we may render *to daimonion* to begin with—with Aristodemos. Socrates started the conversation because he had observed that Aristodemos not only did not sacrifice nor use divination but even ridiculed those who did. Socrates gives no sign of indignation, which in this case would have been quite appropriate, while he was rather indignant—truly or feignedly—in his conversation with Xenophon about kissing a handsome boy. He first found out that Aristodemos admired some human beings on account of their wisdom, i.e., that he did not regard himself as supremely wise, and then that he admired as wise in epic poetry most of all Homer, in dithyrambic poetry Melanippides, in tragedy Sophocles, in sculpture Polykleitos, and in painting Zeuxis. We may remember here that Aristodemos is the transmitter of what was done and said before, during and after the banquet presented in Plato's *Symposium*, in the only Platonic dialogue that presents a comic poet (Aristophanes) and a tragic poet (Agathon) and that ends with a conversation between Socrates and the two poets. In his conversation with the Xenophontic Socrates, Aristodemos is characteristically silent on comedy. (Comedy, which is never mentioned in the *Memorabilia*, is mentioned in the *Oeconomicus*). It is perhaps more important to note that Aristodemos says nothing of his admiring any legislator or other political man for his wisdom.

After he has made sure that Aristodemos admires as wise above all certain kinds of human makers, Socrates asks him whether the makers of animals possessing sense and activity are not more worthy of admiration than makers of images lacking sense and motion. Aristodemos replies in the affirmative but adds the qualification that the animals must not have come into being by some chance but through design. In the context this means that Aristodemos, who finds the customary practices of piety ridiculous, is even uncertain whether there are any gods: he is guilty of that radical impiety of which Socrates was suspected (cf. I.1.5 and 2.31).

Aristodemos grants to Socrates that things manifestly useful come into being through design. Thereupon Socrates shows him that the human senses—the sense of touch is the only one not mentioned (cf. I.4.6 and I.4.12, end)—and other parts of the human body are manifestly useful to man. Socrates speaks here of him who from the beginning made men; i.e., assuming that the human species (and the other species of animals) have come into being, he jumps to the conclusion that there is a single maker; while beginning to speak of men only, he tacitly goes over to animals in general. Aristodemos therefore draws the conclusion that the things mentioned seem to be the work of a wise artificer who loves animals in general. Socrates turned therefore to a different argument; just as the human body contains only a tiny part of the earth, the water, and so on, that exist, it stands to reason that the human intellect is only a tiny part of the intellect that exists or there is a superhuman intellect ordering the immensely great and innumerably many things that are not ordered by the human intellect. This argument points to a world-mind rather than to an artificer of animals. Hitherto Socrates and Aristodemos had spoken of the deity only in the singular; now Aristodemos says, "I do not see the lords as I see the artificers of the things that come into being here." Does he think that the world-mind and the artificer of animals are two different beings? Or does he mean that proving the existence of the world-mind does not in any way prove the existence of the gods? Socrates disposes of this difficulty with his customary ease. Aristodemos raises the further objection that the divine (*to daimonion*) is too grand to need his service. But, Socrates rejoins, since despite its grandeur it deems it worthy to serve Aristodemos, he ought to honor it all the more. Yet Aristodemos does not see that the divine serves him; he declares now his willingness not to neglect the gods if he believes that the gods care about man. Socrates shows him that the gods do care about man by speaking of the splendid privileges which they have bestowed upon men's bodies and souls. This reasoning does not satisfy Aristodemos. In the parlance of our theological tradition, he feels that the requirements of piety are not met by general providence but only by particular providence. In other words, the gods whose existence has somehow been established by Socrates are not necessarily the gods worshipped by the city. To Socrates' question about what the gods would have to do to make Aristodemos believe in their caring about him, he replies, "When they send, as you say that they send to you, counselors as to what one should do or not do"; sending such counselors who advise the individual as to what is good or bad for him here and now (cf. IV.6.8) belongs to particular providence. From Aristodemos' answer it appears that he, who was one of those who lived constantly with Socrates, did not believe in Socrates' *daimonion* despite the fact that Socrates foretold to many of his companions what they should do or not do on the ground that the *daimonion* foretold to him what the outcome would be in the case of compliance or noncompliance (I.1.9): he must have interpreted Socrates' prophetic utterances as non-demonic, as due to human wisdom only; he may have interpreted Socrates' references to his *daimonion* as ironic (cf.

Symposium 8.4; for a not altogether dissimilar case see Plato, *Apology of Socrates* 37e3 ff.). One may say that Aristodemos' unbelief in Socrates' *daimonion* was the root of his impiety. At any rate the present conversation, devoted to *to daimonion*, is devoted also and especially to Socrates' *daimonion*. Taking into account Aristodemos' doubts, Socrates in his rejoinder is silent about his *daimonion* and speaks only of the kind of divination used by the Athenians, the Greeks, and all men; by speaking of the Athenians and the Greeks he keeps, as it were, to a mean between general providence and individual providence. He goes on to ask Aristodemos whether he believes that the gods would have planted in men the opinion that they are able to help and to hurt if they were not able to do it, and that men, deceived all the time, had never found out the truth. But he succeeds somehow in meeting Aristodemos' difficulty by interpreting the world-mind, which is, as it were, the soul of the world-body, as the god's eye and his prudence, which in one act sees and takes care of all things. Yet all this does not yet prove that the gods hear everything and in particular that they hear men's prayers and inquiries; it does not even prove that the gods hear anything and therefore that men must be careful in what they say. Therefore Socrates goes on to say that Aristodemos must in addition worship the gods and try to find out whether they will counsel him about things not manifest to human beings; only then will he come to realize that the divine is so great and of such a character as to see everything, to hear everything, to be present everywhere, and in one act to take care of all things. The gods must hear everything if they are to listen to the myriads of myriads of men who pray to them at any given time; the gods' hearing must receive all those prayers and never be filled. If, as Socrates had said before, man's hearing can receive all sounds and is never filled, his hearing is the most godlike of all senses: it is the sense through which we receive traditions about the gods or from the gods (I.4.6; III.5.9–10). Xenophon does not say anything as to whether Aristodemos was satisfied nor that he henceforth sacrificed and used divination. This is all the more remarkable since the conversation was meant to show that Socrates could not merely exhort to piety but lead to it and into it. Yet Xenophon concludes the chapter with the remark that in his opinion by saying these things Socrates brought it about that his companions abstained from unholy as well as unjust and from base things not only when they were seen by men but also when they were alone. This salutary effect was achieved by the belief in the gods' being able to do good and evil, which, modified by the belief in divine omniscience and justice, becomes the belief in divine reward and punishment. Socrates had not proved that the gods are just or concerned with men's justice.

I.5. Xenophon treats here continence nondialogically. He had treated nondialogically first piety (I.3.1–4) and then presented dialogues on continence and on piety; the two dialogues are surrounded by two nondialogues.

The present discourse is meant, just like the preceding one, to serve as material for judging whether Socrates succeeded only in exhorting men to virtue and in particular to continence or whether he was also able to lead them, at least to some extent, into it. Socrates addresses an indeterminate multitude of male human beings on the subject that continence is a noble and good possession for a male human being; it is not said that the addressees were companions of Socrates, i.e., men who lived constantly with him.

Socrates shows by three examples how undesirable incontinence is; the examples are those of a general, an executor of

a last will, and slaves of various kinds; since incontinence is undesirable even in slaves, must not everyone guard himself
against becoming incontinent? While greed is thought to be
harmful only to others but helpful to oneself, incontinence is
harmful to others but still more so to oneself; greed is compatible with continence and perhaps even calls for it (cf. also
Oeconomicus XII.11–16). Incontinence is likewise undesirable
in friends, i.e., in men associating not in order to transact
private or public business. In sum, one must believe that continence is the foundation for virtue and establish it before
everything else in one's soul: continence is not in itself a virtue
since it can also be the foundation of greed, i.e., of injustice.
In accordance with this Xenophon opens the chapter with
the conditional clause "If continence is a noble as well as a
good possession for a man." In a different context (IV.3–5)
Socrates will suggest that one must establish in one's soul piety
and justice prior to continence; here he suggests the opposite.
This sheds light retroactively on the conversation with Aristodemos. Socrates goes further. Swearing, like a woman, by
Hera, he expresses the opinion that a free man ought to wish
not to obtain an incontinent slave and an incontinent man
ought to pray to the gods to obtain good masters, for only by
obtaining such masters could he be saved. Socrates seems here
to admit that one ought to pray not only for the good things
in general, the gods knowing best what kind of things are
good (I.3.2) but also for certain good things since their goodness is manifest to man: which of the two contradictory
speeches of Socrates is true? Xenophon does not say that by
making such speeches on continence Socrates made people
continent. He only says that Socrates showed himself even
more continent in his deeds than in his speeches. How one can
show oneself continent in one's speeches, appears from Xeno-

phon's deeds in the *Memorabilia;* he puts a limit to what he is
prepared to say, and in doing this he imitates Socrates himself.

I.6. Socrates' continence is not indeed the theme but the
starting point of the conversation which the sophist Antiphon
imposed on him in order to draw away from him his constant
companions (*synousiastai;* the term occurs only here) who
were present at the conversation; the conversation is the only
one with a man called by Xenophon a sophist. Xenophon, de-
viating from his custom, indicates that he reports literally what
Antiphon said. Antiphon believed, as he said, that those who
philosophize should grow in happiness; but Socrates had become miserable through philosophy, and, being a teacher, is a
teacher of miserableness (*kakodaimonia;* cf. *Clouds* 102–4 and
503–4). The facts by which he supports his condemnation can
all be reduced to Socrates' unusually great continence and endurance; although Antiphon does not speak explicitly of continence and endurance, he refers in particular to Socrates'
continence regarding money (cf. I.5.6). Socrates defends his
way of life on the whole along the lines suggested by Xenophon in the preceding chapters. It appears that Antiphon is as
much dissatisfied with the Socratic way of life as were Kritias
and Alkibiades (I.2.16) but he is apparently not a man of political ambition. Socrates mentions to Antiphon this additional
consideration: his continence regarding the pleasures of the
body stems from his awareness of a more lasting pleasure,
namely, the pleasure going with one's belief that one is successful in one's work or that one is growing in virtue (cf.
IV.8.6). He traces the difference between Antiphon and himself to Antiphon's believing that luxury and extravagance is
happiness whereas he holds that to need nothing is divine and
to need as little as possible is nearest to the divine. Perhaps
Socrates quotes here tacitly from one of Antiphon's writings

(Hermann Diels-Walther Kranz, *Die Fragmente der Vorso-kratiker* [7th ed.; Berlin: Weidmann, 1934–1937], 87B10).

There were two more conversations between Antiphon and Socrates. At the first of them, i.e., at the central conversation, Xenophon was clearly present; it is not equally clear whether the other constant companions were. Antiphon said that Socrates' not taking money for his companionship is tantamount to admitting that he does not know anything of any worth and proved that he is just but in no manner wise. Socrates replied that men who sell their wisdom for money to anyone who wishes are compared by us (respectable Athenians) to male prostitutes and called sophists while we hold that anyone who teaches someone whom he knows to be well-fitted by nature whatever good he possesses and thus gains a good friend, acts as a gentlemanly citizen should; as others take delight in a good horse, or a dog, or a bird, in the same way and even more so Socrates takes delight in good friends; if he possesses anything good he teaches it and he commends those friends to others by whom he believes they will be benefited to some extent in regard to virtue; the treasures of the wise men of old which they have left behind in their writings—the treasures are not the writings—he reads together with his friends and if they discover in them something good, he and his friends cull it; they regard it as a great gain when they thus become friends. Xenophon adds that when he heard this Socrates seemed to him to be blessed and to lead the hearers to gentlemanship.

We understand now the purport of the chapter: it presents Socrates' continence as the foundation for his happiness, for his whole way of life; the chapter is the only chapter of the *Memorabilia* that is devoted to Socrates' way of life as a whole. His way of life is presented here as culminating, or his wisdom is presented here as consisting, in his discerning study together with his companions of the writings of the wise men of old. How this activity is related to Socrates' always conversing about the "what is" of the human things is not stated by Xenophon but perhaps there is no need for its being stated. Xenophon underlines the importance of the Socratic utterance which he reports here by calling Socrates here and nowhere else "blessed" (*makarios*). He does not give a single example of his master's blissful activity; this is a further example of his continence in speech.

We must pay attention to the distinction between good friends and friends in general: good friends must be gifted, i.e., able and eager to share in the blissful activity mentioned; a friend need not be more than an old acquaintance with whom one is in a relation of mutual benevolence; only the former are truly friends.

In the third conversation Antiphon asks Socrates how he believes to be able to make others political men while he himself does not engage in political activity. Socrates replies that he could in no way engage in political activity to a higher degree than by taking care that as many as possible are fit to be politically active. This contradicts Xenophon's earlier statement to the effect that Socrates' associates were unpolitical men (I.2.48). That statement was difficult to reconcile with the fact that Socrates was teaching the political things. What we learn now also does not agree with the earlier statement referred to. Perhaps we should say, as we ventured to suggest earlier, that Socrates had two kinds of "companions": those who had political ambitions and those who had not. We just came across a similar distinction, the distinction between Socrates' good friends and his friends in a vague sense. It would be a grave, not to say fatal, error to believe that the two distinctions are identical: when Xenophon spoke of Socrates' true associates (I.2.48) he did not say that they were gifted men.

The sequence "piety-continence" was not imposed on Xenophon but merely suggested to him: why did he choose it? The whole section deals with "the man himself"; the virtues which he fails to discuss here are justice, courage, and wisdom. As for justice, the whole *Memorabilia* is devoted to it; courage is not counted among Socrates' virtues. We suggest then that the conversation with Antiphon deals with Socrates' wisdom: the central conversation refutes Antiphon's assertion that Socrates is not wise.

I.7. This discourse is only meant to supply material for judging whether Socrates exhorted his companions to be concerned with becoming virtuous; it is not meant to show that he led them to or into virtue. Did he exhort his companions to virtue by dehorting them from boasting? He showed them that one makes oneself at least ridiculous by boasting of skills or qualities that one does not possess, by striving for a good "image" while neglecting one's becoming good. One does not merely make oneself ridiculous but one commits a fatal error by boasting that one is fit to rule a city or to be in charge of any other hazardous work without being fit for it. He gives all together seven examples. He does not mention the false pretense to wisdom which can easily be found out and he does not mention the false pretense to justice for another reason. He does not speak in so many words of the very common form of boasting which consists in claiming to know what one merely believes.

The discourse causes a difficulty less by its content than by its place. Someone might say that the speech against boasting—which can be taken to imply that Socrates was the opposite of a boaster—follows the speech showing that he was not extremely miserable (*kakodaimon*) because these two reproaches of Socrates are mentioned together in the *Clouds* (102–4). This explanation is not sufficient because it does not take into account the plan of this whole section (I.3–II.1). As we have seen, Xenophon tries to follow here the plan of the indictment by speaking repeatedly first of piety and then of continence, I.6 being a most important supplement to the preceding chapter that is explicitly devoted to continence. I.5 and I.7 are nondialogic speeches; the first is devoted to continence; what is the theme of the second? The chapter following the speech against boasting is again devoted to continence: could the speech against boasting deal in a disguised way with piety? Could impiety be a kind of boasting? To be sure it could, but what could have prevented Xenophon or Socrates from saying so? The preceding conversation on piety was devoted more precisely to *to daimonion* (I.4.2) and it dealt also and especially with Socrates' *daimonion*. Could Socrates' speaking of his *daimonion* be an act of boasting? By speaking of his *daimonion* Socrates could easily seem to claim that he was more privileged by the gods than any other man (cf. IV.3.12). At his trial he "talked big" to his judges and this "talking big" included his raising his claim regarding his *daimonion* (*Apol. Socr.* 2, 13–14, 32). Socrates had an unusually keen power of perception and therefore also of "divining" the fate of his companions; he referred to his *daimonion* whenever he did not wish to give a reason for his conduct or for his advice, or in order to give his reason an apparently unassailable support. If this is so, I.6 is devoted to Socrates' true superiority and I.7 to his apparent superiority.

II.1. This chapter is again devoted to Socrates' exhorting his companions to continence. Xenophon mentions seven respects in which one ought to be continent. The interlocutor is Socrates' companion Aristippos. The occasion for the conversation was Socrates' being aware that Aristippos was rather incontinent in the seven respects. The point of view from which continence and incontinence are to be discussed is the question of how one would educate on the one hand a young man so that he will be able to rule and on the other hand a young man so that he will not even lay claim to rule. It appears without difficulty that the future ruler must be continent while the young man of the opposite kind may well be incontinent. Socrates speaks in apparently unnecessary detail of the mortifications and dangers to which adulterers expose themselves quite unnecessarily since there are so many opportunities to relieve oneself of one's sexual desires. Certain it is that Aristippos agrees fully and simply with Socrates' assertion that adultery is foolish. But neither he nor Socrates says that committing adultery is incompatible with being fit to rule. Is he thinking of Alkibiades' adventure with the Spartan queen? Alkibiades certainly was not altogether unfit to rule despite his incontinence. Or, to take an example which Xenophon mentions, the younger Cyrus was a man fit to rule and had intercourse with the wife of the ruler of Kilikia (*Anabasis* I.9.1 and 2.12; cf. *Oeconomicus* IV.19). A man committing adultery may be more fit to rule than very many very continent people. When Socrates asks Aristippos into which of the two classes of men or of young men he puts himself, he replies without hesitation that he does not put himself at all into the class of those who wish to rule. He justifies his preference, not by his incontinence but by the extremely troublesome character of ruling; the cities deem it right to treat their rulers as he treats his slaves; he belongs to the class of those who wish to live as easily and pleasantly as possible. Socrates asks Aristippos next whether the nations, or cities, which rule live more or less pleasantly than those which are ruled. Aristippos seems to be embarrassed by this question which would seem to call for the answer that the rulers live more pleasantly than the ruled. Since he had rejected ruling as unpleasant, he would have to say that ruling is less unpleasant than being ruled. He frees himself from this embarrassment by saying that he chooses a middle way between the way through ruling and that through subjection, namely, the way through freedom, the way that leads in the highest degree to happiness. Socrates replies that the middle way would be viable if it did not lead through human beings; living among human beings one must either rule or be ruled by force or by voluntary subjection, for the stronger understand how to use the weaker as slaves. In other words, if one is not willing to play the hammer, one must play the anvil; human life is necessarily political. This applies to societies as well as to individuals; among the individuals too the manly and strong subject and exploit the unmanly and weak. To avoid subjection and slavery, Aristippos does not confine himself to any political society but lives everywhere as a foreigner. This is in Socrates' view a marvellous trick; Aristippos only over-looks the fact that the citizens protect one another against the suffering of injustice and nevertheless do not escape com-pletely from what they fear; how will a solitary foreigner like Aristippos live in safety? It appears that a man living like Aristippos is exposed to an unusually high degree to the in-justice of others; it does not appear that he himself is an unjust man. It is true that as he lives now, no one will wish to en-slave him since he is wholly useless as a slave; but masters would know how to cure him of his incontinence and laziness. Socrates reminds Aristippos of how he treats his slaves. He thus invites us to be amazed at his inconsistency; he is set on leading an entirely unpolitical life while he makes use of a political institution; it was for the same purpose that he had mentioned earlier that Aristippos belongs to the Greeks. Aristippos has the impression—it is only in this context that he addresses Socrates by name—that Socrates holds the kingly art (i.e., the exercise of that art) to be happiness; he still does not see how the rulers or citizens who voluntarily undergo deprivations and hardships of various kinds differ from those who suffer these evils through necessity, except that the former are foolish. Socrates refutes him by the consideration that he who voluntarily abstains from food and drink for instance can eat and drink whenever he wishes, which is not so in the case of him who abstains of necessity, and he who undergoes toils voluntarily does it gladly in the hope of the rewards which he expects thus to obtain—rewards like the acquisition of good friends, the overcoming of those he hates, admiration of himself, and praise and emulation by the others; the acquisition of "friends" as distinguished from "good friends" is not a sufficiently alluring reward.

"Furthermore, the avoidance of exertions and the pleasures of the moment are unable to bring the body into a good condition, as the gymnastic trainers say, nor do they put into the soul any science worth mentioning, but the cares exercised with endurance make one attain noble and grand deeds, as the good men say." One would expect Socrates, or Xenophon, to tell us whether there are not any men who say that the way of life praised by Aristippos does not put into the soul any science worth mentioning and who these men are, just as he identified the trainers on the one hand and the good men on the other; it is safe to assume that the omitted central class consists of the philosophers. The good men whom he has in mind and whom he quotes in the immediate sequel are Hesiod, Epicharmos, and Prodikos the wise. Their statements differ from what had been said by Aristippos or Socrates because they trace the

necessity of toiling to the gods; they give theological support
to the Socratic recommendations which lack such support.

The quotation from Prodikos, which fills almost half of the
chapter, is not literal; it is less magnificent than the original.
It describes Herakles' education by Virtue. The quotation
from Prodikos follows two quotations from Epicharmos, who
had treated Herakles' voracity comically. Prodikos, who was
not famous for his continence and endurance, refers as little to
a tradition or an authority as Protagoras does in telling his
myth in Plato's *Protagoras*. When Herakles reached adoles-
cence, he did not know whether he should choose the way
through virtue or the way through vice. Then two tall women
appeared to him who obviously had come up to him together,
the one in a most decent posture and parure and of obvious
decency, the other looking and behaving like an expensive
prostitute clad in a multicolored dress, adorned by all kinds of
cosmetics, and in addition degraded by incredible vanity. The
latter rushed up to Herakles and promised him, if he would
only choose her, to lead him to the most pleasant and easiest
life; he would not have to give any thought to wars, troubles,
and toils and would enjoy all kinds of sensuous delights. She
is called Happiness by her friends and Vice by those who hate
her: no one calls her Misery. Meanwhile the other woman
had come up; knowing his parents and his nature, as it had
revealed itself in his upbringing, she promised him that he
would become an excellent doer of noble and high things provided he would act according to the manner in which the gods
had disposed the beings, i.e., the good and bad things—Vice
had been silent on the gods just as she had been silent on
Herakles' parents; the good things—the favor of the gods, love
by friends, honor by a city, admiration for virtue by all
Greece, abounding harvests, wealth from cattle, victory in

war, bodily strength—are acquired by exertion, service, and sweat; Virtue replaces admiration of oneself by admiration for virtue by all Greece. While Vice had not mentioned any benefit accruing to her from Herakles' joining her, Virtue expects from it a considerable increase of her prestige. While Herakles had asked Vice for her name, he does not ask Virtue for hers.

To a mischievous interruption by Vice which is explicitly traced to Prodikos, Virtue replies by nobly if severely rebuking her competitor. (For Virtue's characterization of Vice compare Socrates' characterization of Prodikos in Plato's *Protagoras* 315d4–6.) Vice is an immortal being but cast out by the gods and despised by the right kind of human beings; the most pleasant of all sounds, praise, she has never heard, and the most pleasant of all sights, a noble deed of her own, she has never seen. Her followers live a dissipated and lazy life in their youth while a hard and strenuous life awaits them in their old age. Virtue on the other hand lives in the company of gods and good human beings. No noble deed, divine or human, is performed without her. She is honored more than anyone else among gods and among good human beings, of the greatest help to artisans, masters of households, slaves, in the toils of peace and the deeds of war, and in friendship. Her friends are dear to the gods, beloved by friends, and precious to their fatherlands. By toiling hard Herakles may acquire the most blessed happiness. While Vice is a fallen goddess, nothing is said of Virtue being a goddess at all: the gods do not lead a life of hardship and deprivation. But only through Virtue's company will there be noble deeds of gods. At the end Socrates asks Aristippos to consider Virtue's or Prodikos' lesson with a view to his own life. Xenophon does not report whether or in what sense Aristippos was moved by the beautiful speech.

The good men praise the life of hard work, of noble deeds,

the way of life culminating in the kingly art which, as it
seemed to Aristippos, Socrates regarded as happiness. This way
of life has its foundation in continence. But there is another
way of life which also has its foundation in continence, the
way of life through which science is put into the soul and
which culminates in Socrates' blissful activity; about this way
of life "Prodikos" (to say nothing of "Epicharmos" and
"Hesiod") is altogether silent. In other words, at the crossroads
at which Herakles was wooed by Virtue and Vice, not two
but three ways meet: the mere fact that the way of life of the
gods is neither the way of life of Virtue nor that of Vice
shows that there is a third way or, to borrow Aristippos' expression, a middle way. One must also not forget Xenophon
himself, who for some time at any rate led the life of a stranger,
which however in his case was not simply unpolitical. The
twofoldness of the ways discussed by "Prodikos" is as incomplete as the twofoldness of the Speeches which are commis-
sioned by Socrates to state their cases in the *Clouds:* Socrates'
logos is neither the just *logos* nor the unjust *logos*. The middle
way recommended by Aristippos may be as impossible as Socrates says that it is, but the Socratic middle way is viable.
Aristippos opposes the simply unpolitical life, the way of life
of a man who is everywhere a foreigner (the *xenikos bios;*
see Aristotle, *Politics* 1324a14–17), to the simply political life;
but there is a third way of life which is neither simply political
nor simply unpolitical. (For the distinction between the two
virtuous ways of life see in particular *Oeconomicus* XI.)

The exhortation to continence with a view to its being indispensable for a future ruler can hardly have induced Aristippos to practice continence or even to wish to be continent. If
this is so, the conversation can have been useful only to the
other companions of Socrates, or else it is not even an exhorta-

tion at all but meant to shed light on political virtue and therewith on the political life.

The expressions used by Xenophon at the end of I.7 (*toiade*) and at the beginning of II.1 (*toiauta*) would ordinarily suggest that II.1 is a dehortation from boasting and I.7 is an exhortation to continence. It is easy to see how the conversation with Aristippos could be a dehortation from boasting: Aristippos' claim that he lived more happily and securely as a foreigner than as a citizen is an act of boasting. The harangue in which Socrates dehorts from boasting is an exhortation to continence since it draws our attention to the continence which Socrates displayed by speaking of his *daimonion*.

Let us summarize what we have observed regarding the plan of this section: I.3.1–4 deals nondialogically with piety; I.3.5–15 deals (chiefly) dialogically with continence; I.4 deals dialogically with piety; I.5 deals nondialogically with continence; I.6 deals dialogically with continence and the Socratic way of life; I.7 deals nondialogically with boasting; II.1 deals dialogically with continence.

Relatives

Let us call "editorial remarks" statements of Xenophon which vouch for the authenticity of the Socratic discourse reported in the chapter in question ("I have heard him say," "I know," and the like), or which indicate whether the discourse is or is not literally reported, or which indicate whether Xenophon was present on the occasion. The chapters devoted to relatives contain no editorial remarks. Xenophon does not even indicate that II.2 opens a new section or that II.2–3 forms a new section. The two chapters are also silent on the effect of Socrates' admonitions.

II.2. Socrates had noticed that his oldest son Lamprokles

was angry at his mother. To help him, he makes him first agree
that ingratitude is unqualifiedly unjust. The agreement is based
on the common opinion about ingratitude and especially on
Lamprokles' opinion that ingratitude even to foreign enemies
is unjust. He then applies the result to the relation of children
to their parents: there are no greater benefactors than the
parents; hence ingratitude to parents is the height of injustice.
The parents are such great benefactors of their children in the
first place because they bring them from not-being to being;
how great a good being alive, i.e., the enjoyment of the beautiful and good things bestowed by the gods on the humans, is, is
shown by men's clinging to life and fearing death. One cannot
say of course that children are only the by-products of the
parents' satisfying their sexual desires; for such satisfaction
does not require marriage. Socrates says nothing to the effect
that in generating children the parents think to provide for
their old age (*Oeconomicus* VII.12). In choosing their wives
men are visibly guided, not by their sexual desire, but by their
concern with the excellence of the expected offspring. The
husband provides his wife and children with the most abundant
means of support that he is able to provide. The wife does
much more for the offspring; there are not only the troubles
and dangers of pregnancy but also the many maternal cares
for the child after its birth. Both parents do everything to
provide their children with the best possible education. Lamprokles does not question that his mother has done all the
things enumerated by his father and very many other things
besides; but this does not make her ill-temper any more en-
durable; he finds her savagery even less bearable than that of a
wild beast. He must admit that she never beat and kicked him
but she says things to him about him which no one ever
wished to hear for anything in the world because they cause

him shame. Socrates draws his attention to the terrible things which actors in tragedies say to one another without getting angry at one another. But, Lamprokles replies, they do not mean what they say: does your mother mean it? Socrates thus convinces Lamprokles that his mother has good-will toward him; he does not speak of course in the present context of the inadequacy of good-will (cf. I.2.52). Instead he speaks of the care his mother has given him especially when he was sick and of her praying on his behalf for many good things and her performing vows: and you complain about her ill-temper. It is safe to say that the prayer of Socrates' wife differed from Socrates' standard prayer (I.3.2); her prayers were her substitute for knowledge. He then makes him admit that one must try to gain the good-will of everyone with whom one comes into contact by pleasing him and doing service to him: all the more must he do service to his mother, namely, in order to regain her good-will temporarily lost. The only kind of ingratitude which is punished by the city is the ingratitude to parents or the neglect of them both in their lifetime and after their death. From all this it follows that Lamprokles ought to ask the gods for forgiveness if he has acted in any way wrongly regarding his mother; otherwise the gods too might consider him ungrateful, hence would not expect him to be grateful to them for any favors they might bestow upon him and hence not bestow them. Similarly he must fear to be regarded as ungrateful by human beings.

As on other occasions one must pay attention not only to what Xenophon says but also to what he does not say. His Socrates does not for a moment consider it wise to talk over his son's complaint with his wife: Xanthippe's bad temper is a phenomenon like bad weather against which speech is of no avail. The only thing that can be changed, and even be changed by speech, is the posture of those who have no choice but to undergo the bad weather.

One of the charges against Socrates was that he subverted the authority of the fathers. One might expect or at least wish to read a discourse by which Socrates led back, or tried to lead back, a rebellious son to due respect for his father. There is no such discourse. Lamprokles never calls Socrates "father."

II.3. This is the first conversation between Socrates and one of his true associates mentioned by name in I.2.48. Chairephon (cf. *Clouds* 102–4; Plato, *Apol. Socr.* 21a3 and *Charmides* 153b2), one of these associates, it appears, was as difficult a brother to Chairekrates as Xanthippe was a difficult mother to Lamprokles. In both cases Socrates talks to the human being who suffers from his difficult relative and not to the difficult relative herself or himself. But whereas in the first case it could not with propriety be made clear why Socrates did not talk to the difficult relative, it could be done with the greatest propriety in the second case: custom demands that Chairekrates, being the younger brother, take the first step toward reconciliation. Chairekrates knows that Socrates is in the habit of following custom. The only relatives thematically discussed in the *Memorabilia* are difficult people; this shows the soundness of the view that blood relations, as distinguished from friends, are "the necessary ones" (II.1.14); they are not freely chosen. It throws some light on the true associates of Socrates, as distinguished from "his good friends," that Xenophon calls Chairephon and Chairekrates "acquaintances" of Socrates.

Chairephon and his only brother Chairekrates once were quarreling. Socrates points out to Chairekrates the great advantages which brothers may derive from one another. Chairekrates, who grants what Socrates had said in general, thinks that it is not applicable to his case, given the defective character of his brother, and regards their dissension as irremediable. Socrates finds out from Chairekrates that his brother is quite obliging to others; precisely this is so galling to him. Chairekrates vigorously denies that Chairephon's conduct toward him is due to Chairekrates' unintelligent handling of him: it is all Chairephon's fault, who tries everywhere to annoy him by speech and deed. Socrates cannot refer here, as in the case of Lamprokles, to the great benefits which he owes to his difficult relative. Instead he must speak of the arts and spells by which men appease angry dogs or captivate human beings. He compares the proper relation of two brothers to the cooperation of the two hands, the two feet, the two eyes, and the like: in both cases the god has made the pair for their mutual support. But not all men have a single brother. Socrates speaks as if only to have a single brother, not more nor less, were natural.

Friends

The section on friends is divided into general exhortations to or regarding friendship (II.4–6) and conversations and narratives showing Socrates' conduct toward his friends (II.7–10). There is no such division in the section on relatives where the general exhortations are integrated into the conversations that show Socrates' helpful conduct in regard to relatives. More precisely, the conversation with Chairekrates deals with the proper conduct of relatives but it does not deal with Socrates' helpful conduct toward his relatives. His helpful conduct toward his relatives is presented only in the conversation with Lamprokles. The section following the section on friends deals with those who yearn for the noble things (III, beginning), i.e., in the first place for political offices. This implies that the friends are a class different from those yearning for the noble things; this is in agreement with what was suggested in I.2.48.

There are no general exhortations to strive for the noble things as there are general exhortations regarding friends in the section on friends.

II.4. This chapter begins as indirect discourse; only in the second half does it turn into direct speech. Nothing is said to the effect that the speech is addressed to, or occurs in the presence of, "companions" (*synontes*); this chapter and that which follows are the only chapters of the *Memorabilia* that begin with "I once heard him say . . ." The speech is in Xenophon's opinion most helpful for the acquisition and use of friends. Socrates contrasts the praise by the many of a good friend as a very great good with their conduct, with what he sees people do as distinguished from what he hears them say: they care much more about their slaves, i.e., a part of their possessions, than about their friends. And yet a good or honest friend is a most useful and fruitful possession. The friend is considered strictly from the point of view of the useful: the very word *kalos* in any of its forms or uses does not occur in this chapter. Socrates praises here "the good friend"; but "good friend" too has more than one meaning. Neither here nor in the whole section does Socrates even allude to his most blissful activity through which he and his friends became friends. In the preceding conversation he had compared a pair of brothers to the pair of hands, the pair of feet, and the pair of eyes made by the god for their mutual benefit; now he compares to the paired parts of the body a pair of friends; the friendships most highly praised in song are those of two (*Symposium* 8.3–6; Aristotle, *Nicomachean Ethics* 1171a14–15); what is not true of brothers is perhaps true of friends. The allusion to the pair of friends is an allusion to the highest kind of friendship. In speaking of friends here Socrates does not refer to the gods.

II.5. This chapter continues the theme "the friend as useful property" by discussing the various prices of friends. One of Socrates' companions had neglected Antisthenes, who was pressed by poverty; Antisthenes was also a companion of Socrates (III.11.17) although he is not described as such here. Socrates asked Antisthenes in the presence of the neglectful companion and of many others, among them Xenophon, whether there are prices of friends as there are prices of slaves; some slaves are very cheap, others of a middling value—among them those who fetch a price equal to Socrates' monetary worth (*Oeconomicus* II.3)—and others very expensive. Antisthenes answered heartily in the affirmative. Socrates drew the conclusion that if this is so, one must examine himself with a view to one's own value to one's friends and try to become as valuable as possible. One betrays worthless friends just as one sells worthless slaves. This seems to be a warning addressed to the neglectful companion that he should cease to neglect Antisthenes; it seems to be an attempt to correct the neglectful companion. In fact it justifies him: no one neglects a valuable friend. Was Antisthenes then not a valuable friend, and in particular not a valuable friend of Socrates? Surely he was not *the* friend of Socrates (cf. *Symposium* 8.31); that place of honor was reserved for Plato.

The low view of friendship is stated by Socrates not merely when he talks to mere acquaintances but also when he talks to companions: the companions consisted of a great variety of human beings, low and high.

II.6. The two preceding chapters dealt with the lowest kind, or aspect, of friendship; the present chapter deals with friendship among gentlemen. The interlocutor is Kritoboulos, the son of the true associate Kriton. We have met Kritoboulos together with Xenophon in I.3 where Xenophon was the interlocutor; it is not made clear whether Xenophon was present at the conversation recorded in II.6; Kritoboulos may have reported it to Xenophon. Xenophon was present when the highest kind of friendship, the kind connected with Socrates' blissful activity, was discussed, just as he was present when the lowest kind of friendship was discussed. There is a connection between the themes "friend" and "Xenophon": what kind of friend of Socrates was Xenophon?

The explicit theme of the chapter is how to test what sort of friends are worth acquiring. Socrates asks Kritoboulos how one would begin to inquire if one wished to acquire a good friend. They dispose at once of the incontinent; the respects in which men are incontinent are stated in the usual manner (cf. I.5.1 and II.1.1). They also easily agree that five other kinds of men are undesirable as friends, for instance, those greedy for money and therefore driving a hard bargain and those who are quarrelsome or factious. Kritoboulos then raises the question as to how one could make a friend of a man meeting the indicated requirements. Socrates replies that one must first find out whether the gods counsel one to make him one's friend or, as Kritoboulos puts it, whether the gods do not oppose it; Kritoboulos would regard the gods' ambiguous silence as unambiguous approval. This is the only passage in the section on friends where the gods or the god are mentioned (I disregard the oaths); reference to the gods or the god occurred as a matter of course in the section on relatives. We may note in this connection that piety is not mentioned among the qualities which a man desirable as a friend must possess, just as it was not mentioned in Socrates' conversation with Aristippos about the qualities of a man fit to rule. It is no less important that reasonableness (*phronesis*) or an equivalent is not mentioned among the qualities of a potential friend as he should be, although this quality is indispensable in a friend according to Socrates (I.2.52–53).

Kritoboulos next asks how one should hunt for friends. Socrates replies that one must do it through incantations and spells. A model of an incantation is the way in which the Sirens addressed Odysseus. Socrates' use here of a passage from the *Odyssey* reminds us of his use of another passage from the same poem in the sentences preceding his conversation with Xenophon which took place in the presence of Kritoboulos and on his behalf. But now when Socrates converses with Kritoboulos, Xenophon has no opportunity to note the playful character of Socrates' interpretation of a Homeric passage (cf. I.3.7–8). In other words, incantations are manifestly not sufficient. (This is indicated by the contrasting of the solid achievements of Themistokles with the spells used by Perikles.) What Socrates says leads Kritoboulos to surmise that according to him only through becoming good oneself in speaking and doing can one acquire a good friend. Socrates asks him whether he believes that a man who is the opposite of good could acquire useful and respectable friends. He replies that he had observed worthless orators being friends of good public speakers and men incompetent to lead an army being close to men very skilled in strategy. Socrates admits that Kritoboulos' observation is correct but denies that it is relevant to their conversation. Kritoboulos misunderstood Socrates by surmising that only through becoming good in speaking (a good orator) and in doing (a good general) can one acquire a friend good at speaking and doing. There is a kind of friendship in which the two partners are of very unequal worth, for instance, the friendship between Socrates and most if not all of his friends—Socrates can be the friend of wholly unphilosophic men—but this kind of friendship is not the subject of the conversation. Socrates has in mind friends who are useful to one another in a wide sense of "useful," and a wholly un-military man can obviously be most useful to a first-rate general. Kritoboulos grants that useless men are unable to acquire useful friends, or, as he rephrases this admission, that a bad man cannot acquire gentlemanly friends but, he worries, will one, after having become a gentleman, easily be a friend to the gentlemen? What disturbs Kritoboulos is the fact that gentle-men frequently are the very opposite of friends to one another —they frequently belong to different factions—and, as he adds, even the cities which are to the highest degree concerned with the noble things are frequently hostile to one another. Considering these things he is greatly discouraged regarding the acquisition of friends; obviously the bad are by nature enemies rather than friends to one another; nor can the bad be friends to the good; but if the men practicing virtue fight for precedence in the cities and envy and hate one another, where among human beings will we find friendship, good-will and trust? Socrates shows Kritoboulos a way out of his predica-ment by first stating that human beings have by nature things leading to both friendship and hostility. In other words, it is as wrong to say that men are by nature good as to say that they are by nature bad. Socrates' statement applies equally to non-gentlemen and to gentlemen, the gentlemen being led to hostil-ity, as we have seen, in particular by desire for superiority and therefore also by envy. Nevertheless, Socrates asserts, friend-ship slips through these impediments and unites the gentlemen, for thanks to their virtue they desire only moderate posses-sions, they are continent despite their taking delight in the sexual enjoyment of youths in their bloom, and, above all, they take away envy entirely by regarding their own and their friends' good things as common. Hence it is plausible that the gentlemen should be able to rule jointly to their common benefit. One of the benefits the gentlemen derive from ruling is that they thus can help their friends within the bounds of justice. "Friend" and "gentleman" are two different things; every friend may have to be a gentleman, but not every gentleman is a friend. Nevertheless, nothing prevents a gentleman from engaging in political activity after having made the best men his friends; it is surely preferable to having them as one's opponents; in addition, it is easier to benefit the best, who are few and less in need, than the worse, who are many and demand many benefactions. The minority of gentlemen if they are friends can easily keep down the majority consisting of nongentlemen. The gentleman is, or should be, a political being; in fact he supplies perhaps the solution of the political problem. But political friendship and friendship simply are two different things.

There still remains therefore the question as to how one can make a gentleman one's friend. Socrates says that since he is erotic, he might be able to assist Kritoboulos in his hunting for a friend. According to Xenophon, Socrates' speaking of his erotic desire was playful (IV.1.1-2). Socrates himself does not say this of course. We note that Socrates uses erotic language in his conversation with Kritoboulos, whom he had so severely rebuked for having kissed a handsome boy; when considering that passage (I.3.8-13), we felt that Socrates' indignation was playful. Socrates is erotic because of the passionate character of his desire to be loved in turn by those whom he loves, to be longed for by those for whom he longs, and to be united with them by a reciprocal desire to be together. Kritoboulos wishes to be loved by gentlemen, i.e., beautiful (noble) and good men, by men good in regard to their souls and beautiful in regard to their bodies. Both Socrates and Kritoboulos make clear, each in his way, the difference between a gentleman in general and a gentleman who is desirable as a friend. (Cf. *Oeconomicus* VI.16).

Socrates' knowledge or science—erotics—does not have the power to make everyone whom Kritoboulos loves love him in return. It can only prepare such a result. Socrates refers again to the Sirens as his model. The Sirens, as distinguished from the Skylla, allured all men—they do not allure men anymore—by charming them from afar: Kritoboulos may allure men by letting Socrates act on his behalf. Socrates says now that the Sirens sang to all and charmed all while he had said previously that they sang to, and charmed, only those who are eager to be honored on account of their virtue. He traces the present version to what people say while he had traced the first version to Homer. The difference may have to be traced further to a difference in the meaning of virtue. If Kritoboulos desires the friendship of someone, Socrates will tell him that Kritoboulos admires him and wishes to become his friend. He will also with Kritoboulos' permission praise Kritoboulos as having all the makings of a good friend, in particular by having realized that a man's virtue consists in surpassing his friends in helping them and his enemies in hurting them. That this is a man's virtue follows necessarily from the necessarily political character of man's life or from its grounds. The striving for superiority is by no means eradicated but channeled so as to support friendship. Socrates does not speak here of the virtue which he possessed or strove for—a virtue which does not include the desire to surpass his enemies in hurting them (cf. IV.8.11). Socrates cannot say more in praise of Kritoboulos—for instance, he cannot say that Kritoboulos in fact surpasses his friends in helping them and his enemies in hurting them—since by doing so he would do Kritoboulos all the harm which boasting does to the boaster. Only within these limits, Kritoboulos notes, is Socrates his friend. In what sense Socrates regarded Kritoboulos as his friend, can best be seen from the *Oeconomicus* (cf. III.12). As appears from the present context, Kritoboulos was skilled neither in strategy nor in acting as a judge nor in being a statesman, nor even in the management of a household. Whether he became good at managing his household through the conversation recorded in the *Oeconomicus* is another question.

At the end of the conversation Kritoboulos indicates that in his view something may be noble without being true and vice versa.

To summarize, the conversation on friendship among gentlemen moves from the primary view according to which the gentleman is simply the good man to a deeper view which questions the supremacy of the gentlemen in the ordinary meaning of the term while granting that rule of the gentlemen thus understood supplies perhaps the solution to the political problem; it would solve it if there were a sufficient number of true gentlemen in a given city. The interlocutor in this chapter is also the interlocutor in the *Oeconomicus*, the secondary but central subject of which is the perfect gentleman.

II.7. Here begins the subsection which is meant to show that Socrates tried to cure the difficulties of his friends which were due to ignorance by judgment and the difficulties which were due to want by instructing them to assist one another according to their power. This implies that the three preceding chapters did not deal with the difficulties of Socrates' friends, except accidentally. Kritoboulos in particular was not in a difficulty, at least not in a serious one.

Socrates once saw Aristarchos looking sad and asked him to tell him his troubles. Socrates did not have any knowledge of his troubles (see the *akousas* after Aristarchos' report). Aristarchos cannot have been one of Socrates' constant companions. His troubles were due to the war and the civil war and more directly to the many female relatives who had found refuge in his house, fourteen of them; he did not see how he could feed them in the circumstances. Socrates finds out that Aristarchos' relatives do not work for the very good reason that they are gentlefolk; they could do various kinds of useful things but doing them would be beneath them; it would befit slaves or craftsmen. Socrates points out to him that it is not very becoming nor healthy to do nothing except to eat and to sleep; the ladies that do nothing except to eat and sleep are more useless than slaves or craftsmen and hence inferior to them. As matters stand, there is a very great danger that Aristarchos and his relatives will come to hate one another—he because he regards them as only a burden and they because they see how annoyed he is with them. On the other hand, if he puts them to work, to do the useful things which they know how to do, everyone will be satisfied. He followed Socrates' advice. He raised capital—it is not clear that he did this on Socrates' advice—purchased wool, and set his ladies to work; everyone was happy. The only inconvenience that resulted was that the relatives reproached Aristarchos for being the only one in the house who ate without working. Thereupon Socrates advised him to tell them the speech of the dog. At the time when animals could speak, the sheep complained to the master that they produced many useful things and got nothing except what they took from the land, while the dog, who did nothing comparable to what the sheep did, got his food from the master. To this, not the master, but the dog replied, "By Zeus, I protect you against men and wolves." The relatives correspond to the sheep, Aristarchos corresponds to the dog, but who corresponds to the silent master? The Platonic Socrates swears from time to time "by the dog"; the Xenophontic Socrates only makes a dog swear "by Zeus."

II.8 The interlocutor here is an "old comrade" of Socrates whom he once met after not having seen him for some time. Socrates asks him whence he comes; he does not ask him about his troubles because he does not look troubled. And yet Eutheros has lost all his property as a consequence of Athens' defeat and must now earn his living by the labor of his body; he preferred this to asking anyone for help. Socrates does not advise him to ask one of Socrates' friends nor does he ask one of his and Eutheros' friends to assist him: Eutheros does not belong to the circle of Socrates' friends. The narrator Xenophon does not mention here the name of the interlocutor nor that of Socrates. Socrates warns Eutheros that he will not be able for long to earn his living by the labor of his body; he ought to seek at once from some more prosperous man a different kind of work for which he would be fit also in older age. But Eutheros does not like servitude. Socrates enlightens him by saying that the political leaders also serve and yet are regarded as men doing the work befitting free men to a higher degree than those who do not so serve. Socrates disregards the difference between public service and private service. It is hard to find a pursuit in which one does not have to serve human beings. Nothing is said as to whether Eutheros took Socrates' advice. It does not appear that Socrates despite his poverty ever worried about the source of his livelihood in old age.—This is the only chapter in this subsection in which we are left in the dark about the outcome.

II.9. The interlocutor here is Kriton, one of Socrates' true associates. Kriton once complained to Socrates about the troubles caused him by sycophants. Comparing Kriton's property to sheep and the sycophants to wolves, Socrates suggests to him that he should get and keep someone who would do to the sycophants what the dogs do to the wolves, i.e., a counter-sycophant who would never think of turning against Kriton. In this case, as distinguished from that of Aristarchos, it is clear who is the master. In this case Socrates does not leave matters at giving Kriton sound advice; he joins Kriton, or Kriton joins him, in the search for a suitable man; they find Archedemos, very capable of speech and action but poor. Kriton made him gifts and did all the other necessary things. Archedemos liberated Kriton from the sycophants who were glad to give Archedemos money in order to avoid criminal prosecution. Archedemos did the same service to Kriton's friends, regardless of whether they had asked for that service or not. When a sycophant reproached him with flattering Kriton because he was being benefited by him, he replied that it is hardly base to benefit gentlemen by whom one is being benefited and to make them one's friends. Certainly Archedemos became one of Kriton's friends and was honored by the other friends of Kriton. Did Socrates honor Archedemos? At any rate Kriton, the friend of Socrates and of Archedemos, had very different kinds of friends. Xenophon helps us in making the necessary distinctions by refraining from speaking in this chapter of "good friends"; he only speaks of good dogs. He does not call Kriton a friend of Socrates.

II.10. Unless we believe that Archedemos was Socrates' friend before Socrates and Kriton approached him, the present conversation is the only one in the subsection which shows how Socrates alleviated his friends' difficulties that were due to want by instructing them to assist one another. Yet the interlocutor is Diodoros, a "comrade" of Socrates, and Hermogenes, whom he is asked to help, is an "acquaintance" of Diodoros and one of Socrates' true associates (I.2.48). Socrates reminds Diodoros of the care which he invests when one of his slaves runs away or is sick: all the greater care should he invest in helping Hermogenes, who is in danger of perishing from want and who in return would do him services surpassing in value the services of many slaves; good managers of households buy valuable things when they can be bought at a low price; but owing to the present state of things one can acquire good friends at extremely small expense. Following Socrates' advice Diodoros went to Hermogenes and acquired him as a friend without spending much.

In the case of his true associates Kriton and Hermogenes, Socrates did more than give them advice. One may therefore say that the movement from II.7–8 to II.9–10 is an ascent. Yet the strictly economic character of the advice given to Kriton and especially to Diodoros compels us to say that precisely these two conversations mark an extreme contrast to what Socrates says about his acquiring friends when speaking of his blissful activity. In the light of that statement the difference between Kriton and Archedemos becomes indeed insignificant.

Men Longing for the Noble Things

This section is the only one whose subject matter is explicitly stated by Xenophon.

This section, just like the preceding one, consists of seven conversations. The noble things are identical or almost identical with high offices in the city; the men longing for the noble things are at least primarily men of political ambition. At the beginning of the section Xenophon says that Socrates helped those longing for the noble things by making them take trouble about what they longed for: he did not encourage political ambition itself. We were told in the refutation of the charge

that Socrates' true associates were precisely those free from
political ambition (I.2.48; cf. II.9.1). In accordance with this
Xenophon vouches for the authenticity of most of the conversations on friends, while he vouches for the authenticity of
only one of the conversations with the men longing for the
noble things. But we were also told that Socrates took care that
as many as possible should become capable of doing the political things (I.6.15). Yet being capable of doing the political
things and longing for political office are not identical.

The interlocutors in the first three conversations of this section are nameless. The interlocutors in the following four conversations are men bearing characteristic or even famous names
or who were connected with famous men. The connection between political honors, fame, and name is obvious. It seems that
the movement in this subsection has the character of an ascent.

III.1. When Socrates had heard that Dionysodoros had come
to town professing to teach generalship, Socrates persuaded one
of his companions of whom he sensed that he wished to obtain
the office of general in the city, to take lessons from Dionysodoros, for, he said, since so much depends for the city on the
quality of its generals, a man who is careless about learning
generalship, while caring very much for being elected general,
is criminally negligent. The young man went to Dionysodoros,
learned what he taught, and came back. Thereupon Socrates
greeted him jokingly by saying to the others who were present
that his very looks now show him to be a general, for since
he has learned generalship, he is henceforth a general, even if
no one ever elects him; knowledge of generalship, not election
or the practice of generalship makes a man a general, just as
knowledge of medicine, not election or the practice of medicine makes a man a physician. The Socratic joke implies that
the young man need no longer care to be elected general nor

to desire to practice generalship. The thesis that generalship is knowledge reminds us of the thesis that virtue is knowledge: does the virtuous man not have to practice virtue?

Socrates finds out from the companion that Dionysodoros taught him only tactics. But tactics is only a very small part of generalship. Among the other things which a general must be able to do Socrates mentions that the general must be kind and cruel, straightforward and devious, lavish and grasping; he must possess many qualities both by nature and by knowledge. Courage is not explicitly mentioned, perhaps because it must be common to the general and many of his subordinates. Generalship is not simply knowledge; at the very least, the knowledge that a general must possess can be acquired only by men who are by nature gifted for it. Owing to the fact that a man's virtue consists in benefiting his friends (fellow citizens) and inflicting harm on the city's enemies, the general's character must be ambiguous; he must be good to his soldiers and bad to the enemy. He must not be simply kind and simply cruel; he must use kindness or cruelty as the circumstances require. This however means that he must know how to use them: knowledge regulates the use of the various opposite qualities. (From the view that generalship requires the prudent alternation between niceness and nastiness, there is not a very long way to Machiavelli's view that government requires the prudent alternation between moral virtue and moral vice.) Socrates does not deny the importance of tactics. He compares a well-ordered (*tetagmenon*) army to a finished house in which all parts are in their proper place; the materials that neither rot nor decay are placed below and above and the other materials in the middle. The companion finds this likeness very apt: in war too one must put the best in the front and the rear and the worst in the middle.

We have noted more than once in the *Memorabilia* and else-where that the item which is literally in the center is of special importance. It was a rule of forensic rhetoric to discuss the strong points of the defense in the first part and in the last part and the weak points in the center, i.e., when the attention of the listeners is flagging. The weakest points are the most important in a speech or book that presents an unpopular or forbidden view in the guise of a perfectly innocent or "ortho-dox" view; in such a book the innocent things come to sight first and last; such books are to some extent products of for-ensic rhetoric. This statement about the crucial importance of what is in the center is very general; it must be read in the light of the examples; those examples are of a great variety. As Socrates puts it to the young companion: there are many cases in which one ought not to arrange or lead (speak) in the same manner. The *Memorabilia* as a whole offers a conspicuous ex-ample of an exception.

Socrates finds out that Dionysodoros taught even tactics very imperfectly. He asked the companion therefore to return to the teacher and to ask him for further instruction, for if he knows and is not impudent, he will be ashamed to send you away without that knowledge after having taken your money: Socrates is silent on whether Dionysodoros can be expected to return the money if he does not possess the knowledge in ques-tion; being a general of sorts, he is a thief of sorts. Socrates could have given that instruction himself but he tactily refuses to do so. If he possessed the knowledge which a general needs, he was a general without ever having learned generalship, with-out even having desired to be a general, and without ever practicing generalship.

III.2. This chapter presents a Socratic statement addressed to an elected general who remains silent. He is a general by virtue of election; nothing is said about his competence, and in particular about his knowledge or his having learned generalship. The statement is the most general statement about generalship, kingship, or leadership that occurs in the *Memorabilia*. No playfulness is visible here; the elected general is obviously not a companion of Socrates. Following Homer, Socrates compares the relation of the general to the soldiers with that of the shepherd to the sheep: just as the shepherd must take care that the sheep are safe and sound, that they get what they need, and that the purpose for which they are fed is achieved, so the general must take care that the soldiers are safe and sound, that they get what they need, and that the purpose for which they campaign is achieved; he does not state the purpose for which the sheep are fed, because this would unbalance the comparison; he states of course the purpose for which men campaign. On the basis of a Homeric verse Socrates contends that the people elect a king with a view, not to the happiness of himself alone, but to the happiness of the electors as well. But at the end the virtue of a good leader proves to consist in making the led happy: the good leader forgets his own happiness. It is therefore not easy to find something more noble than generalship: it is not impossible. The question as to what induces a man to become a leader is not raised here, any more than the question of what constitutes the happiness of the led. The final silence on the happiness of the general corresponds to the silence on his knowledge. That final silence corresponds also to the silence on the bliss of Socrates' hearers as distinguished from the bliss of Socrates himself (I.6.14).

III.3. Xenophon vouches for the authenticity of this conversation of Socrates with a young man who had been elected cavalry commander. Xenophon is the author of a treatise on the skill of a cavalry commander. The conversation begins with Socrates' addressing to the young man the very question which was not raised in the preceding chapter: why did he desire to be a commander? He does not have a ready answer but he replies in the affirmative to Socrates' question about whether his purpose was to benefit the city. But in order to benefit the city, one must possess the necessary competence. The young man believes that it is not his business to improve the horses; when Socrates shows him his error, he readily agrees. He seems to know that he must improve the horsemen but he does not seem to know that he must excite the souls of the horsemen and arouse their anger against the enemies, nor how he can make them obedient to him. Socrates explains to him that in every business men willingly obey those whom they think to be best at it, i.e., in each kind of work the knowers; hence the cavalry commander must come to sight as the one who knows best what is to be done. But knowledge is not enough; he must also be able to teach the horsemen that obeying him is both more noble and more salutary for them. To the young man's surprise this means that a cavalry commander must also be an able speaker. Socrates mocks him by asking whether he believes that one should command cavalry by silence. He then embarks on a speech setting forth that the things most noble by law or otherwise are taught by speech, that those who teach best use speech to the highest degree and those who understand the most serious things to the highest degree converse (*dialegontai*) most nobly. At the end of the conversation Socrates exhorts the cavalry commander to try to exhort his men to those things from which he will be benefited and through him his fellow citizens. Love of the city becomes most effective through one's desire for praise and distinction; praise and distinction constitute the specific happiness of the military commander. In the case of this particular elected commander it is not clear whether he should have been elected.

This is one of the few chapters in which Socrates swears prior to the interlocutor and at the same time swears more frequently than he.

III.4. In the two preceding conversations the interlocutors were men elected to military command; Socrates did not state an opinion on their election. In the present conversation, where the interlocutor is a man not elected to the office of general, Socrates defends the election of his rival and therewith the Athenians at whom the defeated man was angry. Socrates' loyalty to the regime appears in a favorable light, but of course generals were not elected by lot. Nikomachides was angry because he was not elected, not because of his victory-promising name, but despite his military achievements including wounds received in battle, the scars of which he exhibits to Socrates as proof of his worthiness. Instead of him the Athenians elected Antisthenes, who had no military achievement to speak of (but he was a knight) and who understands nothing but how to amass wealth. Socrates defends the Athenians' choice on the grounds that Antisthenes because of his money-making ability will be able to provide the soldiers with supplies and above all that he loves victory: all the choruses of which he was in charge won in the competitions; he had no experience in song and choruses and yet was able to find the men best at these things; he will be able to find the men best at fighting without doing any fighting himself; he will be more willing to spend money on winning victory for the whole city in war than on winning a choral victory for his tribe. Nikomachides cannot believe that in Socrates' view the same man can be a good *choregos* and a good *strategos*. Socrates makes his meaning clear by enlarging his thesis: over whatever a man presides—be it a chorus, a household, a city, or an army—he is a good president if he both knows what is needed and is able to provide it. Knowledge is not enough; in the case under discussion wealth is also necessary. Nikomachides would never have believed that Socrates would say that good householders would be good generals; the good presidents of choruses are silently dropped. While Nikomachides' rival knows nothing to speak of of choruses, he is a good householder. Socrates suggests that they examine the actions of the householders and the generals in order to see whether they are the same or differ in something. Nikomachides grants to Socrates that the householder and the general have many important things in common but fighting, he says, is peculiar to the general. Socrates denies this: both have enemies and for both it is useful to overcome their enemies. Nikomachides retorts that in the fighting itself the art of household management is of no use. Socrates denies this too: the good householder who knows that nothing is as profitable and as gainful as to defeat foreign enemies by fighting and nothing as unprofitable and entails as great a loss as to be defeated, will eagerly investigate and procure what is conducive to victory and carefully consider and guard against what leads to defeat. Again we see that knowledge is not enough. So Socrates concludes with an admonition that would deserve to be used as a motto of a large volume setting forth the principles of what has been called the dismal science: Do not look down, Nikomachides, on the economic men, for the management of private things differs only in size from the management of public things, but in the other respects they are similar and in particular in the most important respect that neither can be carried out without human beings nor is one of them carried out through different human beings than the

other; those who know how to use the human beings prosper
in both private and public affairs.

Socrates reaches this result by abstracting from the qualita-
tive difference between the public and the private. It is most
obvious that he disregards the fact that generals are elected and
managers of households are not. This difference is due to the
fact that the military and political ruler, as distinguished from
the householder, rules free adult males, i.e., his equals. Denying
the essential difference between the political ruler and the
householder is tantamount to denying the importance, the
truth of equality and of freedom in the political sense. (This
explains why the conversation with Nikomachides is the central chapter of this section.) That denial is implied in the assertion that knowledge, and not election, makes a man a ruler.
To return to the surface, Socrates abstracts from the specific
dignity, grandeur, and splendor of the political and the military,
from what Homer meant when he called Agamemnon "ma-
jestic" (III.1.4; cf. also the *Iliad* quotations in III.2; in the section on friendship—II.6.11—the *Odyssey* is quoted. Homer is
never mentioned in the *Oeconomicus*.) This is in accordance
with the inclination of the Xenophontic Socrates to deny that
there is a difference between the good and the noble. The
denial of an essential difference between the "political" and the
"economic" could be thought to reconcile the statements according to which Socrates' true associates did not go into politics and Socrates took care to enable as many (companions) as
possible to become political men (I.2.48 and 6.15). Yet not all
true associates of Socrates were good managers of households;
there is a great difference between the wealthy Kriton and the
poor Hermogenes; there is a great difference among Socrates'
true associates. We should also mention that the "economic"
understanding of the political was prepared for by the "eco-

nomic" understanding of friendship (see especially II.10.4) which minimizes the difference between slaves and friends almost as much as Socrates in speaking to Nikomachides minimizes the difference between the manager of the household and the general.

If there is no essential difference between the good general and the good statesman on the one hand and the good householder on the other, the question of Socrates' military and political competence can be reduced to the question of Socrates' competence as economist; this important question forced upon us by the *Memorabilia* can be answered only by the study of the *Oeconomicus*.

III.5. Conversing once with Perikles, the son of the very Perikles, Socrates said to him that he hoped that now after he had become general, the city would become better and more famous regarding the affairs of war, and would vanquish her enemies. Socrates apparently approves again of an election by the Athenians. Perikles replied that he wished for the things Socrates had said but did not know how they could come about. Socrates asked him whether he wishes that they should by arguing (*dialogizomenoi*—the word ocurs only here in Xenophon's Socratic writings) about these matters consider in what way they are feasible; Perikles wishes it. Their exchange leads first to the result that the Athenians are equal or superior to the Boiotians in five points; the third point is that Athenians are friendlier among themselves while many of the Boiotians are ill-disposed to the Thebans who treated them badly; the last point is that no people can boast of greater and more numerous noble deeds of their ancestors than the Athenians. Yet, Perikles objects, since the two great defeats which the Boiotians inflicted on the Athenians, the Athenians themselves regard themselves as inferior to the Boiotians. Socrates is aware

of this great change but expects consequences salutary to the
Athenians from the Boiotians' self-confidence and the Athenians' fear: fear makes men more attentive, more obedient, and
more amenable to good order, as one can gather from how
sailors behave when they are afraid of a storm or enemies, as
distinguished from their behavior at other times. Perikles raises
again an objection to the apparently too sanguine Socrates:
granting that the Athenians are now willing to obey from fear,
fear is not the same as passionate desire for ancient virtue,
fame, and happiness. Socrates refers him to the similarity of
(hence to the difference between) the desire for wealth and the
desire for pre-eminence conjoined with virtue: if we wished
to make the Athenians desirous of the wealth of others, we
would show them that it is their patrimony and belongs to
them; since we wish that they concern themselves with pre-
eminence conjoined with virtue, one must show them that their
pre-eminence belongs to them from antiquity, and by making
every effort to regain it they will surpass all. One would show
this by reminding them that their most ancient ancestors of
whom we know through hearsay were, as they have learned
from hearsay, most excellent. Perikles wonders whether Socrates means the judgment in respect to the gods which Kekrops
and his men gave because of their virtue. Socrates means it indeed although it was Perikles who spoke of it. This is the only
mention of gods that occurs in this section. (Cf. the only mention of the gods in the section on friends—II.6.8—where Socrates brings up the subject and Kritoboulos treats it perfunctorily.) The mention of the gods is in harmony with the praise
of antiquity, the ancestors and the paternal that pervades the
whole conversation. While Socrates meant the judgment about
the gods, he dwells at some length on the other great deeds of
the Athenian heroes of the most ancient antiquity and, with less

emphasis ("if you wish"), on the great deeds performed by the Athenians not so long ago, i.e., in the Persian war. This praise of antiquity, of the remote or not so remote past, to which Perikles assents is in striking and silent contrast to the great Perikles' preferring the achievements of his generation to those of the generation of the Persian war and still more to those of the still earlier ancestors (Thucydides II.36). The younger Perikles wonders how in the world the city ever declined; the Periklean age is tactily described as an age of decline. The earlier contrast between the spellbinder Perikles and the solid achievements of Themistokles (II.6.13) implied already this much. Socrates traces Athens' decline to the city's self-neglect and carelessness which followed almost inevitably her great achievements. In other words, just as the Boiotians are now endangered by their self-confidence and the Athenians are after their defeats in a better shape owing to their fear, the self-confidence of the Periklean age was already a sign of decline. Yet tacitly tracing the defects of contemporary Athens to the great Perikles among others, Socrates opposes to that Perikles' praise of Athenian daring and light-heartedness a praise of sobering fear, of a quality thought to be Spartan rather than Athenian (Thucydides II.39.4, 40.3, 41.4, and 43.1). Just as in reading Ischomachos' report to Socrates of the admonitions with which he saturated his wife, one sometimes wonders whether the admonitions are addressed to his wife or to Socrates, in reading Socrates' conversation with the younger Perikles, who is of course addressed "O Perikles," one must play with the thought that Socrates addresses his famous father.

Perikles asks Socrates how the Athenians could recover their ancient virtue. They could do it, Socrates replies, either by taking up their ancestors' pursuits if those pursuits can still be discovered or else by imitating those who are now pre-eminent and their pursuits and if possible following these pursuits with still greater care than the men or cities which are now in the lead; a surpassing of the ancestors is not even considered. Perikles despairs of the possibility of discovering and hence of recovering the pursuits of their ancestors; hence he speaks only of the alternative. He, not Socrates, is the one who identifies those pre-eminent now, i.e., the Spartans, explicitly. He contrasts with the loose habits of the Athenians the admirable habits of the Spartans, who reverence their elders, respect their fathers and rulers, train their bodies, live in concord without envying one another more than foreigners, do not waste their time in litigation, and do not treat the public things as if they were alien to them (cf. Thucydides I.70.6). For all these reasons he is always in great fear that some evil past endurance may befall the city. Socrates is now again in the enviable position that he can defend his fellow citizens, i.e., the established regime, against reproach. He denies that the Athenians suffer from a depravity that is past remedy. He refers to their excellent discipline in the navy, their athletic contests and the choruses. When Perikles rejoins that the lack of discipline of the hoplites and the horsemen, supposedly the noblest part of the city, is therefore all the more deplorable, Socrates reminds him of the still more noble and even venerable Council of the Areopagos—of the same Areopagos whose power had been weakened by Perikles' father (Aristotle, *Politics* 1274a7–8, and *Constitution of Athens* 27.1; cf. Plutarch, *Pericles* 9.3–4). He thus corrects, as far as in him lies, the established regime. Perikles agrees with Socrates' praise of the Areopagos but insists all the more on the deplorable condition of the army. Socrates surmises that this defect may be due to the ignorance of the commanders, for the Athenians obey their rulers in choruses and in athletics because in these endeavors all rulers are able to show where they learned their skill (and hence that they possess the required knowledge), which is not so in the case of most generals; this does not apply to Perikles, who is surely able to say where he learned the general's skill, one reason being that he is the son of a most famous general. Perikles understands that Socrates' praise of his knowledge or of his concern with the acquisition of knowledge is an exhortation to learning rather than a statement of fact. Socrates is silent here about the knowledge possessèd by the generals commanding the navy as the cause of the sailors' good order; he had traced that order before to fear rather than to any knowledge on the part of the commanders, let alone of the sailors. After having alluded to the older Perikles' strategy he returns to the conflicts between the Athenians and the Boiotians with which he had begun. He suggests that by imitating certain barbarians the young Athenians, accoutred with lighter arms, could harm the Boiotians by raiding their land while preventing them from entering Attika. By suggesting that the whole territory be defended against enemy incursions Socrates tacitly opposes the whole strategy of the great Perikles (Thucydides I.143.4–5 and II.13.2; cf. Xenophon, *Respublica Atheniensium* 2.16); this is to say nothing of the radical opposition to the older Perikles' policy that is implied in the silence strictly observed throughout the conversation about the war between the Athenians and the Spartans. If Perikles will follow Socrates' advice, Socrates concludes, this will be noble for him and good for the city: he will earn deserved praise and the city's interest will be well served; his own interest might suffer. As Xenophon tells us in the *Hellenica*, Perikles became one of the generals in command at the victorious battle at Arginusai (and thus earned deserved distinction) and then was condemned to death unjustly and illegally.

III.6. From the height of Perikles we descend without any visible preparation to the folly of a youth whose longing for the noble things was blind ambition. But in order to understand the plan of the *Memorabilia*, its secret law, one must consider not only the qualities of the interlocutors but also and especially the rank of the subject matter. In the present section we observe without difficulty an ascent from purely military matters to the political in the comprehensive sense. In the preceding conversation the primary theme was still military but it appeared that the recovery of Athens' ancient military virtue requires what comes close to a change of the regime, for what characterizes a regime is rather its spirit than peculiar institutions. The two last conversations of this section are simply political. This however means that the larger part of the section devoted to the city, or to distinction in the city, is devoted to military matters. The reason playfully expressed is that *polis* stems from *polemos*. (Cf. Plato, *Republic* 407e2–408a1.)

At about the same age at which the young Alkibiades cross-examined the great Perikles regarding law without making himself in the least ridiculous (I.2.40 ff.), Glaukon, the son of Ariston, tried to address the Assembly, eager as he was to be a leading man in the city, was dragged from the speaker's stand, and made himself ridiculous. No one could stop him; Socrates alone, who was well-disposed toward him for the sake of Charmides the son of Glaukon and for the sake of Plato, stopped him. How he stopped him, Xenophon shows by the present conversation. Socrates gained Glaukon's attention by setting before him the resplendent rewards which he could expect if he succeeded in becoming the leading man in Athens. He asks him then from where he would start benefiting the city, such benefiting being necessary if he wished to become honored. Glaukon is reduced to silence since he had not ap-

parently given any thought to what would be in the language
of our time his first priority. Sensing how Glaukon feels, Socrates asks him whether he would try to increase the city's
wealth just as, if he wished to increase the estate of a friend, he
would attempt to make him richer: increase of the estate or of
the wealth of the city rather than management of the estate or
of the city is for Glaukon of course the goal (cf. *Oeconomicus*
I). It appears that Glaukon had not given any thought to the
present revenues and expenditures of the city; the revenues
might have to be increased and the expenditures to be de-
creased. Glaukon defends himself by having recourse to the
indubitable fact that one can enrich the city at the expense of
the foreign enemies. But only, Socrates warns, if one is stronger
than the enemies. He asks him therefore about the military
power of the city and that of her enemies. Glaukon proves
again to be utterly ignorant. The same result is reached when
he is asked about the defense of the country and the silver
mines. When speaking of the silver mines, Socrates openly
makes fun of Glaukon. (A full explanation of this act would
require an adequate interpretation of Xenophon's writing on
Athenian revenues.) Socrates finally points out to Glaukon his
ignorance regarding the grain supply of the city. He refers
again to the parallel of the city and the household: just as the
manager of the household must know all its needs and take care
that they are supplied, the manager of the city must know all
her needs and take care that they are supplied; but the city consists of more than ten thousand houses: should not a beginner
like Glaukon first try to manage a single household, say, that of
his uncle Charmides, which is badly in need of competent management? Glaukon would gladly try his hand at it but his
uncle will not listen to him: how can you, unable as you are to
persuade your uncle, imagine that you will be able to persuade

all the Athenians, your uncle included, to accept your counsels? Socrates concludes with an exhortation to Glaukon that he should above everything else try to get thorough knowledge of what he wishes to do, for in every field of human endeavor the men most famous and admired come from among those who are the most knowing: knowledge is necessary but not sufficient for fame in the city.

In this chapter Socrates delineates the scope of political knowledge or rather of the political knowledge required of an Athenian statesman. We here see Socrates "teaching the political things." Political knowledge thus understood has, so to speak, nothing in common with the core of Socratic knowledge, with the raising and answering of the "what is" questions, for instance of the questions "What is the city?"; "What is a statesman?"; "What is rule over human beings?" (I.1.16). In a chapter of the *Rhetoric* (I.4) Aristotle enumerates the subjects about which political men deliberate or the subjects of deliberative or political rhetoric. They are: revenues, expenditures, war and peace, military power, defense of the country, food supply, and last but not least, legislation and its relation to the various regimes. The agreement with Xenophon extends to many details. All the more remarkable is Xenophon's silence on the subject mentioned by Aristotle last: it is part of Socrates' justice that he does not discuss the variety and change of laws, as distinguished from obedience to the established laws whichever they may be. This is only confirmed by the manner in which Xenophon presents Socrates' teaching on the variety of regimes (IV.6.12). As for Xenophon's silence on peace here, we simply refer to Glaukon's contribution to the discussion of warfare in the fifth book of Plato's *Republic*.

III.7. Socrates was favorably disposed to Glaukon for the sake of Charmides, the son of Glaukon. Immediately after having reported Socrates' conversation with Glaukon, Xenophon reports his conversation with Charmides. But whereas Socrates had to discourage Glaukon, he had to encourage Charmides: Charmides is the only man whom Socrates encourages before our eyes to go into politics. Charmides was a remarkable man, by far superior in ability to those engaged in politics at the time but hesitant to enter political life. Apparently he is the only one of the seven interlocutors in this section who does not spontaneously long for the noble things. Socrates suggests to him that a man who is able to take care of the affairs of the city and thus to exalt the city and therefore to gain honor for himself but hesitates to do so is soft and cowardly. This applies to Charmides, who, considering his ability, is under a necessity to go into politics since he is a citizen. This remark reminds us of the question as to why Socrates' true associates and above all Socrates himself did not go into politics; it reminds us faintly of Aristippos' praise of the life of a stranger. Socrates has recognized Charmides' ability from the superior judgment which he showed when he talked to the politicians. But, Charmides points out, conversing privately and conversing in public or with the public are not the same thing. Socrates does not seem to see the difference: a man who is able to count, does so no less well in a multitude than when he is alone. Charmides is therefore compelled to remind him of the most obvious and massive things: sense of shame and fear, which are inborn in man and are much more effective in the presence of crowds than in private gatherings. Socrates is now compelled to liberate Charmides from the surely mistaken sense of shame and fear which hold him back, by enlightening him: it makes sense to feel shame in front of the wisest and to feel fear when one is confronted with the strongest but it is absurd to be ashamed to speak before the most unreasonable and weakest men. Charmides is ashamed of these seven kinds of men: the fullers, the shoemakers, the carpenters, the smiths, the farmers, the merchants, and the small traders who think of nothing but buying cheap and selling dear; for all these make up the Assembly (cf. IV.2.22). (As for the central position of the smiths, cf. *Oeconomicus* I.1) Socrates liberates Charmides from his native sense of shame and fear which hold him back from politics by debunking the democratic Assembly; he instills in him what he regards as a justified contempt for the *demos*. (*Demos* occurs only here in the whole section.) Charmides has one argument left: precisely if I am as superior as you say, I may be laughed down by the fools who make up the Assembly. To which Socrates replies: the fools too can be laughed down; you, who can so easily make ridiculous the superior men, can easily make the fools ridiculous. Socrates concludes with the admonition "Know thyself." Charmides lacks self-knowledge in the sense that he does not know his great worth and therefore has an exaggerated view of the respectability of the Assembly. Both Socrates' advice to Charmides to engage in political life and his derogatory remarks to him about the Assembly are known not to have remained mere words: as Xenophon elsewhere indicates, Charmides became a leader in the oligarchic revolt, a fellow worker of the notorious Kritias (*Hellenica* II.4.19; cf. *Symposium* 4.32–33). Socrates, it would seem, was responsible for his going into politics by emancipating him from his original, inbred awe of the *demos*. In the eyes of a loyal democrat Socrates' action could well appear as an act of corruption.

Descent

III.8. Socrates was favorably disposed to Glaukon, the son of Ariston, for the sake of Charmides, the son of Glaukon, and for the sake of Plato. Xenophon adds no patronymic in the case of Plato. It would not be wholly unreasonable to expect that the conversation with Charmides which immediately succeeded the conversation with Glaukon would in its turn be immediately succeeded by a conversation with Plato. But Xenophon knew better; he only points to the possibility of a conversation with Plato; the peak is missing; the ascent has come to an end. Instead he reports a conversation with Aristippos, who has in common with Plato that he is a philosopher, if of a much lower rank than Plato. The conversation with Aristippos turns almost imperceptibly into exchanges with nameless people which come close to culminating and in two cases actually culminate in explicit answers to "what is" questions. The subsection consisting of III.8–9 is at least externally the most philosophic part of the first three Books of the *Memorabilia*. If we do not forget the pointer to Plato, we are compelled to say that with III.8 the descent begins. The descent becomes ever more manifest in every conversation which follows in Book III. This is not to deny that Xenophon still continues treating the theme "men longing for the noble (beautiful) things" in the largest part of the present section: wisdom for which the philosophers long is obviously something noble; painters and sculptors are the makers of beautiful things (III.10); and Theodote, the interlocutor in III.11, is sought after because of her beauty.

It is Aristippos who opens the conversation—Aristippos whom Socrates had tried to persuade to take political life seriously and thus to make him less incontinent than he was (II.1); of his praise of the life of a stranger we were faintly reminded in the conversation with Charmides. The present conversation together with that with the sophist Antiphon (I.6) is the most conspicuous among the very few conversations that are not opened by Socrates.

Aristippos tried to refute Socrates as he had been refuted by him in their earlier conversation. In order to benefit his companions Socrates answered without any fear that his speech would entangle him in difficulties but in agreement with his practice. For Aristippos asked him about the good and the noble. He asked him in the first place whether he knew anything good so that if Socrates mentioned any of the good things, he would show him that the same thing is sometimes bad. But Socrates, knowing that if something annoys us, we need something that will make the annoyance cease, answered that what is good is always good for (or against) something, like fever, disease of the eye, or hunger; as for the good which is not good for something, he does not know it nor need it. Things are good in relation to needs; something that does not fulfill any need cannot therefore be known to be good.

Aristippos then asks Socrates whether he knows anything fine (beautiful, noble, honorable). Socrates knows many fine things. Aristippos asks him whether they are all like one another (for, after all, they are all fine). In doing so he points to the inadequacy of Socrates' answer regarding the good; all good things have something in common; from Aristippos' point of view all good things are good in reference to "living as easily and as pleasantly as possible" (II.1.9 and II.1.11). Socrates refuses to consider this because from his point of view "living as easily and as pleasantly as possible" is not good; he does not wish to make again the futile effort to persuade Aristippos of the goodness of the virtuous life. In addition, Aristippos' answer and any other answer to the fundamental question would not be sufficient for guiding action. Socrates replies to Aristippos' question regarding the fine things that some of them are as unlike as they can be. Yet how can what is unlike the fine be fine? Socrates disposes of the difficulty by two examples accompanied by an oath: a man fine for running is unlike a man fine for wrestling; a shield fine for defense is very unlike a javelin that is fine for forceful and swift hurling. But this reply causes another difficulty for Socrates in Aristippos' view: Socrates has given the same answer to the question regarding the fine as to the question regarding the good. Socrates is surprised by Aristippos' surprise: the good and the fine are the same; all fine things are fine in the same respect, for the same reason for which they are good; everything is held to be fine or good with a view to its usefulness for something. Even men are called both fine and good ("perfect gentlemen") in the same sense. From this it follows that a dung basket is fine and a golden shield is ugly if the former is useful for its purpose and the latter not useful. It follows further, as Aristippos finds out, that the same things are fine and ugly just as the same things are good and bad: what is good for hunger is frequently bad for fever.

As is shown by Aristippos' persistence, the identification of the good and the noble is paradoxical. It is contradicted by Xenophon himself (II.2.3; III.5.28, III.6.30; *Oeconomicus* VI.15–16, VII.15, VIII.18–20). He could not have spoken of "those longing for the good things"—for all men do that—instead of "those longing for the fine things." The paradoxical thesis stems from the attempt to reject the excess of the noble over the good as irrational, just as does the denial of the essential difference between the city and the household (III.4). We may also think of the suggestion of the Platonic Socrates that in a properly constituted city only the most useful marriages are the holy ones (*Republic* 458e3–4). The noble is more problematic than the good. Xenophon devotes twice as many lines to the noble than to the good; in the initial enumeration of Socratic themes "what is noble" occurs in a place of honor and "what is good" not at all (I.1.16).

Xenophon sheds some light on the neglected side of the beautiful in the immediately following speech that is no longer addressed to the hedonist Aristippos, who does not like to endure the heat of summer and the cold of winter, but to nameless people, perhaps to the very companions who were present at the conversation with Aristippos. The subject is houses. The same houses are beautiful and useful; Socrates no longer says that they are beautiful and good. A man who means to have a house as it should be must contrive that it be most pleasant to live in and most useful; now it is pleasant that the house be cool in the summer and warm in the winter; the house must be built accordingly. In a word, a house in which one could escape heat and cold in the most pleasant manner and the belongings would be kept in the safest manner, can be supposed to be the most pleasant as well as the most beautiful domicile; paintings and decorations deprive one more of delights than they afford. Socrates here first replaces "beautiful" by "pleasant" and distinguishes the pleasant from the useful and in particular from what affords safety; he then replaces "useful" (or "safe") by "beautiful." He has no use for beautiful things which do not jibe with the specific pleasure or usefulness expected from the artifact in question.

Finally Socrates speaks of two particular structures, temples and altars. The most becoming location of temples and altars is one which is both most visible and "untrodden"; for it is pleasant to offer one's prayers at the sight of them and it is pleasant to approach temples and altars when one is in an "undefiled" disposition. Socrates does not speak here of the beautiful or of the good; but if anything can illustrate the excess of the beautiful over the good (useful), this example can.

One could think that if the good is the same as the noble and the noble is the same as the pleasant, the good, the noble, and the pleasant are the same, if not simply, at least in the most important case (cf. Aristotle, *Eudemian Ethics*, beginning). Whether Xenophon meant anything like this, remains to be seen.

In the conversation with Aristippos Socrates swears three times and Aristippos never. In the first conversation with Aristippos, only Aristippos swore.

III.9. From the good and the noble, to say nothing of the pleasant, we are naturally led to the virtues; up to this point the order of subjects is more lucid than in the enumeration of Socratic topics at the beginning (I.1.16). The subject now taken up first is courage, which is treated separately from the other virtues (cf. Plato, *Laws* 963e) and which is not called a virtue. Socrates is asked whether men become courageous by teaching or by nature. He replies that some men are by nature more gifted for courage than others but both kinds of men increase in courage by learning and above all by practice. Accordingly courage would belong to the class of things which among human beings are called virtues (II.6.39). But Socrates does not say here that courage is a kind of knowledge or even that it presupposes knowledge. If one wishes one may say that this is due to the fact that the question "What is courage?" is not raised or alluded to.

Socrates, we are told, refused to separate from one another wisdom and moderation (*sophrosyne*). Knowledge of the noble and the good things and doing (making use of) them are inseparable; a man who knows them and does them is wise and moderate. It seems that while wisdom and moderation are not separable from one another, they can be distinguished from one another; "wisdom" refers to the knowledge of the noble and the good things while "moderation" refers to the doing of them. Yet it is commonly believed that a man may know the noble and good things and still not do them. Accordingly Socrates was asked whether he held that those who understand what one should do but do the opposite, are wise and continent: *sophrosyne* has a wide range of meaning extending from the high and profound moderation of a Socrates to mere self-control regarding the pleasures of the body. Socrates does not object of course to the substitution of continence for moderation. He replies that the people in question are neither wise nor continent or moderate. A wisdom that is ineffective is not wisdom just as a moderation that does not flow from wisdom, is not moderation. From here there is only one step, if not a small one, to saying that justice and every other virtue is wisdom, which could seem to mean that justice, etc., and wisdom are not only inseparable but identical. Yet the distinction is preserved, as appears from the supporting reasoning: (1) everything done through virtue is noble and good; (2) everyone who knows the noble and just things chooses them just as everyone who does not know them cannot choose them. The crucial premise is obviously premise 2; but according to Xenophon's presentation 1 is the crucial premise, i.e., the premise which is much less questionable than the other. Perhaps this is not his last word on the subject.

In the speech about wisdom, moderation, justice, and the other virtues Socrates is silent about the difference between the more and less gifted and, above all, on the need for practice in addition to knowledge and on the essential teachability of virtue.

Instead he turns to the opposite of wisdom, i.e., madness. Madness was introduced as the opposite of moderation (I.1.16) but now we have learned that moderation is wisdom. Madness is not the same as ignorance but the popular distinction between madness and ignorance does not coincide with the Socratic distinction between them. For instance, lack of self-knowledge and belief that one knows what one does not know come close to madness in Socrates' view but not in the popular view. Yet even in the popular view madness is understood as a kind of ignorance. Socrates fails to identify madness with vice. In the light of the Socratic distinction, Xenophon's defense of Socrates against the charge that he subverted paternal authority (I.2.50) becomes even weaker than it originally was.

Xenophon then turns to the only two "what is" questions mentioned in this context that were raised and answered by Socrates: "What is envy?" and "What is leisure?" His raising these two questions draws our attention to the absence of "what is" questions from the discussion of the virtues. To understand the selection of envy and leisure one must consider the context. Envy and leisure are discussed immediately after wisdom and its opposites; they are impediments to wisdom or the quest for wisdom. Envy is defined as pain, not at the misfortunes of friends nor at the good fortunes of enemies but at one's friends' doing well. The fathers of some of Socrates' companions envied him because their sons improved in wisdom thanks to him and thus admired him more than they admired their fathers (cf. *Education of Cyrus* III.1.38–39): they were pained by their sons' doing well, and their sons were their most natural friends. More precisely, the quest for wisdom is, or should be, the common activity of friends, an activity by which the friends increase in virtue (I.6.14). Envy of the friends' progress in wisdom is therefore a sentiment that cannot arise in a reasonable (*phronimos*) man. The use of "reasonable" here may remind us of the fact, deliberately left obscure in the preceding discussion, that the wisdom (*sophia*) spoken of there is in fact reasonableness (*phronesis*) (cf. **IV.8.11**). The Socratic denial of the difference between reasonableness and wisdom follows from the denial of the difference between the good and the beautiful or noble things, among the latter the objects of sight standing out (II.2.3). As for leisure, it is a state, not of abstention from doing, but of doing something rather inferior—a state between the ascent to a higher activity and leisurelessness, i.e., descent from a higher activity; it is in this sense a state of rest. Socrates does not spell out here what is superior not only to leisurelessness but even to leisure.

The foregoing interpretations are not incompatible with an alternative interpretation according to which one would have to refer the two definitions to the gods: are the gods envious? do the gods have leisure?

The explanation of leisurelessness marks the transition from the discussion of wisdom to that of ruling (cf. III.11.16).

After Xenophon has reported Socratic conversations or sayings which are not prima facie political, he reports a single Socratic statement about human rule over human beings. Just as virtue is knowledge, ruling is knowledge. Kings and rulers, he said, are those and only those who understand how to rule; he mentions five insufficient or void titles to rule, election by lot occupying of course the center. It goes without saying that force and fraud do not supply a title to rule. Nor do inheritance or election proper. Yet on the other hand Socrates says nothing to the effect that a man loses his claim to rule deriving from his understanding how to rule if in addition he is elected by his fellow citizens or comes to power in any other way, for instance, by force and fraud. But it is simpler to say that the king or ruler is a man who is able to persuade and therefore does not need a single ally because he can do with any interlocutor or any crowd what he likes (I.2.11 and I.2.14; cf. III.7.4). The difficulty is brought out to some extent by the objection of "someone" who said that the tyrant need not obey the man who speaks well because he thinks well. Here it is implied that the tyrant, as distinguished from the king, can rule well only if he obeys another man: the tyrant does not know how to rule. Socrates replies that the tyrant who disobeys his superior, will be punished, for by disregarding the good advice he will make mistakes. There is, as it were, an unwritten, self-enforcing law that keeps the tyrant within bounds or destroys him (cf. IV.4.24). To another objection by "someone" that the tyrant could even kill the man who thinks well, Socrates replies that by doing so he would kill his best allies and thus bring on his speedy downfall; Socrates finds no difficulty in his being, in certain circumstances, the adviser and hence the ally of a tyrant. This fact also weakens somewhat the case of Xenophon against Socrates' accusers.

The examples of military commanders have warned us against understanding in too simple a manner the identification of rulership with knowledge.

The last sayings of Socrates reported in this chapter concern his opinion about what is the best pursuit for a man. He is asked for his opinion on this subject and replies: doing well. Then he is asked again what he thinks about being lucky. Thereupon he shows how different doing well and being lucky are. He would have left matters at "doing well," which would have been understood by many people as "being lucky." To state clearly what he means, he must apparently be sure that the one to whom he talks does some thinking. This became particularly clear in his immediately preceding statements on tyranny which were elicited by sensible questions. Acting well has nothing to do with being lucky: a man is lucky if without seeking he hits by accident on something which is needed or to be done; but he acts well if he has learned and practiced doing well; in every pursuit—farming, medicine, politics—

those who act well are the best and dearest to the gods. At the beginning of the *Memorabilia* Xenophon had told us that according to Socrates acting well is insufficient since it cannot guarantee what is most important, namely, the desired outcome, and that one is therefore in need of divination. The best farmer can be defeated by unusually bad weather. But if those who act well are dearest to the gods, will they not necessarily be successful? Why is there any need for prayer, even for the short Socratic prayer, and for sacrifices? Does this difficulty not follow already from the omipotence of knowledge which is presupposed when it is said that a man is a good general by virtue of knowledge and that ruling is the same as understanding how to rule? It is at any rate remarkable that being lucky is now limited to the unintended doing of something which is needed or to be done and does not extend to the intended outcome (happiness through marriage) of one's action (marriage). (Cf. I.1.6–9.) There is a connection between men's acting well and their being beloved by the gods; is there any connection between men's being lucky and their being beloved by the gods?

III.10. Xenophon descends from what we may call Socrates' philosophic conversations or sayings in the first place to his conversations with men who possess arts and exercise them as a trade. He reports three such conversations. Xenophon's Socrates conversed with artisans very rarely (cf. *Oeconomicus* VI.13), although more frequently than Plato's Socrates. The first conversation reported by Xenophon of this kind is with the painter Parrhasios, who as such made likenesses of things seen, especially of human beings whose beauty is beyond words or speech (cf. III.11.1); yet for this reason the models and the works of this kind are lower in rank than the best things which come to sight only through and in speech (*Kynegetikos* 12.19).

In considering this and the next conversation one must never forget Xenophon's portrait of Socrates and wonder to what extent a painter or sculptor could equal Xenophon's work, to say nothing of Plato's. In portraying beautiful forms, Socrates says, the painters bring together what is most beautiful in different human beings and thus contrive that bodies look beautiful in all their parts, for it is not easy to come across a single human being whose looks are blameless in every point. Parrhasios agrees. But when Socrates asks him whether the painters imitate the most winning, the most delightful, the most friendly, the most longed for, and the most lovable characters, which are characters of the soul, Parrhasios says that these things cannot be imitated since they lack size, color, and so on and are altogether invisible. Thereupon Socrates reminds him of the fact that human beings look at one another in a friendly or hostile manner and look differently when their friends fare well and when they fare ill; these different looks, Parrhasios admits, can be imitated. From here it is only one step, which Parrhasios easily takes, to the admission that the painters can present through the faces and postures of human beings various if not all virtuous and vicious characters. To Socrates' further question whether it is more pleasant to see human beings through whom the noble, good, and lovable characters come to sight than the opposite ones, he replies that there is surely a great difference between the two. He does not say that it is more pleasant to see portraits of the former.— Socrates does not praise Parrhasios' works.

While Socrates showed Parrhasios that painting can imitate more important things than he did and thought, the sculptor Kleiton does prior to the conversation everything that the sculptor should do. Socrates helped him however to a better understanding of his art. He did not have an answer to the question of how he produces in his statues what most of all leads and allures the souls of human beings through their sense of sight, namely, the statues' appearing to be alive. By enabling him to give an account of his work, Socrates was more useful to him than to Parrhasios, whom he had to guide toward doing the most excellent work which a painter can do.

When Socrates visited the armorer Pistias (which he did more than once) as he had visited Parrhasios and Kleiton, Pistias showed him some well-made breast plates. Socrates praised the invention of breast plates as beautiful. He asked him why he charges more for his breast plates than others do although his are neither stronger nor of costlier material than theirs. Pistias replied that his breast plates are better proportioned. Socrates learns that one can and must make well-proportioned breast plates even for ill-proportioned human bodies, i.e., breast plates which fit the latter. Socrates observes that Pistias does not mean well-proportioned absolutely but relative to the user. He also learns that the fitting breast plates are not the "exact" ones but those which do not hurt in use. The speech about what is and what is not well-proportioned is altogether Pistias'. The difference between what is said about breast plates on the one hand and sculptors and paintings on the other illustrates the difference between the good (useful) and the beautiful: paintings and sculptures which are likenesses or imitations are beautiful precisely because they are of no use but good only to be looked at (cf. II.2.3) and for leading our souls.—Socrates could be useful to Pistias only by praising and recommending him (cf. III.11.3).

III.11. We descend next from male human beings, who are not *andres* in the emphatic sense, to a woman—to the only woman with whom the Xenophontic Socrates ever converses before our eyes. She was once upon a time in Athens, was beautiful, by name Theodote, and belonged to the kind who "are with" everyone who persuades them. She was not together with everyone who wished to be together with her, just as Socrates did not converse with everyone who wished to converse with him (I.6.5); she had to be persuaded: could Socrates be persuaded? The sequel gives an answer to this question. One of those present mentioned her and said that her beauty surpasses speech and also that painters to whom she shows of herself whatever she can in modesty, go to her and use her as a model. Perhaps she was once a mistress of Alkibiades. We must go to behold her, Socrates said, for by hearing at any rate one cannot grasp what surpasses speech. So Socrates and those who were with him went to her: he had not gone to Dionysodoros, the teacher of generalship (III.1), for he could find out everything about him by hearing about him. Xenophon does not describe her and hence we cannot compare her looks with those of the two tall women in Prodikos' tale, Virtue and Vice. She surely was not a Xanthippe, a Diotima, or an Aspasia.

When Socrates and his company entered Theodote's house, they beheld her, who just then was posing for a painter. After the painter had ceased his work, Socrates did not say anything about the painting but said: O men, must we be more grateful to Theodote for having exhibited to us her beauty, or she to us for our beholding her? The decision depends on whether the exhibition is more useful to her than the beholding to Socrates and his company or vice versa. Socrates thus raises a question of justice. Considering among other things that he and his companions desire already to touch what they have beheld and that they will go away rather excited, he reaches the decision that they do service to her and that she receives the service. Theodote understands this to mean that she is more obliged to them than they to her. It is our business to wonder whether it is true that she or he to whom service is done (the higher) is more obliged, or more benefited by, those who serve (the lower) than the lower is obliged to, or benefited by, the higher (cf. III.2). From this question of justice Socrates turns away to looking at Theodote's expensive attire, at her mother, who was dresssed and decked out in no mean manner, at her many pretty and by no means carelessly turned out maids, and at her unstintingly furnished house. He therefore asks her whether she possesses land or an income-producing house or craftsmen. She possesses none of these things. He therefore proceeds to ask her from what she lives. She replies that she lives from the gifts of whoever has become her friend. As appears from the *Oeconomicus*, in which the interlocutor Kritoboulos prodded by Socrates declares that friends are money (I.14), Socrates, who, it is true, did not live in so lavish a style as Theodote, had no other means of support than she; her way of life is to this extent a caricature of Socrates'. Socrates had likened the difference between philosophers and sophists to that between a beloved friend and a prostitute (I.6.13). One might call Theodote a courtesan; she certainly is no prostitute: she must be persuaded. Swearing by Hera, Socrates says that a friend is a noble possession and it is far better to have a herd of friends than a herd of sheep, goats, and cattle (cf. *Oeconomicus* I.14). But does Theodote leave it to chance whether a friend settles on her like a fly or does she herself contrive something like a spider? She has no notion of how she could contrive getting friends or how she could hunt worthwhile men. Hunting friends, Socrates explains to her, is more difficult even than hunting hares, for which one must use a great variety of contrivances. Socrates intimates to her that here as elsewhere art (*techne*) is preferable to chance (*tyche*); Theodote is obviously not an expert. The subject of hunting friends had been discussed in the conversation with Kritoboulos (II.6). But there the discussion was preceded by a discussion of what kind of man is desirable as a friend. The latter subject is not thematically discussed with Theodote: the first quality which a man desirable as a friend must have is continence, in particular regarding sex—a subject not explicitly mentioned now. This does not mean of course that everyone is desirable as a friend for Theodote. To her question, by which contrivance that resembles the use of dogs for driving hares into nets she could hunt friends, Socrates replies that she must get someone who like a dog tracks down and finds for her those who love the beautiful and are wealthy, and drive them into her nets. As she learns from Socrates, her nets are her body and the soul in it; among the doings of her soul that are recommended to her are the concern for her friend when he has fallen sick and the passionate sharing in his joy when he has done something noble. Theodote has not used any of the contrivances recommended by Socrates. But she assents to his assertion that she must approach a friend according to nature or correctly, and not with violence (against nature). For instance, she must not obtrude her favors when the friend has no hunger for them. Since she does not know how to arouse that hunger, Socrates enlightens her about it with great kindness and delicacy. No wonder that she asks Socrates to become her partner in the hunting for friends. Socrates is willing provided she persuades him; the art which she needs above and beyond the *ars amandi* is the art of persuasion; even those whose beauty surpasses speech need speech, the art of speaking, in order to make their beauty useful to them. But Theodote cannot persuade Socrates if Socrates does not teach her first how to persuade him, and this he fails to do. He even declines her invitations to visit her often; jesting about his freedom from business, he says that he has no leisure since he has so much private and public business to attend to. He has no leisure in the strict sense (cf. III.9.9); yet still less does he have business. He intimates the character of the state, which is neither leisure nor business, with a view to her by saying that he has female friends who do not permit him by day and by night to leave them since they learn from his love potions and spells —contrivances through which he brings it about that Apollodoros and Antisthenes (constant companions) never leave him and Kebes and Simmias (true associates) come to him from Thebes. Theodote naturally wishes that Socrates lend her such a contrivance in order to lure him. But he does not wish to be drawn to her; he wishes that she come to him; he assures her that he will welcome her unless a female friend dearer to him is inside. By the female friends he probably means his companions who seek him for the sake of philosophizing; he calls them female for the same reason for which he sometimes swears by Hera. The last part of the conversation shows more clearly than what went before the character of the resemblance between "Socrates and his friends" and "Theodote and her friends": Socrates surpasses Theodote by far in the erotic art of which he is the consummate master and she a complete novice and bungler; he is the true *erotikos* who can make others long passionately to be together with him in speech. Socrates could learn something from a competent breast-plate maker about his art but not from a courtesan about hers and Socrates'. The conversation with Theodote is the only one showing that and how Socrates refused to "be together" with someone who wished to "be together" with him (cf. Plato, *Theages*).

Socrates swears in his conversation with Theodote more often than in any other chapter of the *Memorabilia*. It is not explained how Theodote knew Socrates' name.

III.12. From Theodote we descend to Epigenes, who is a

young companion of Socrates indeed but inferior to her in the most conspicuous respect: Theodote has a beautiful body, while Epigenes is poorly off regarding his body. Socrates exhorts Epigenes to take proper care of his body. To do this is necessary in the first place in respect to war, which the Athenians will start if they will so chance; for there are three dangers to which those who do not have a fit body are exposed: not a few of them are killed or save themselves in a disgraceful manner, while many of those whose bodies are fit save themselves in a becoming manner; many of the unfit are taken prisoners and spend the rest of their lives in slavery, perhaps in the harshest kind of slavery, or being ransomed perhaps for more money than they can afford, live ever after in destitution; many others of them acquire the ignoble reputation of wishing from cowardice to shirk fighting. These considerations apparently made no impression on Epigenes. He looks down on these and similar things, it seems, because he thinks that the good condition of the body is of no importance for thinking; but who does not know that the bad condition of the body makes many men commit great errors in their thinking and debilitates them in their acquisition and preservation of knowledge?

Socrates tries to induce Epigenes to long for the beautiful (noble) things. The conversation with Epigenes which in a way concludes the present section, parallels the conversation with Charmides which concludes the preceding section, inasmuch as both Epigenes and Charmides do not long for the noble (beautiful) things.

III.13–14. The last two chapters of Book III transmit Socratic speeches addressed to nameless people just as did the first three speeches of that Book; yet the speeches reported in the last two chapters were not addressed to companions, while at least the first chapter was. The content of the last two chapters is quite different from everything that went before and that follows. The speeches here convey sensible counsels no doubt, but one would not have to be a Socrates in order to be able to give them: Socrates as Socrates is here completely invisible, even more invisible than in a good portrait or statue. The speeches in III.13 are addressed to people who are in a bad temper or annoyed or worried for trifling reasons. The name of Socrates does not occur here. It also does not occur in some other chapters but the same device may perform different functions; the function which it performs here is indicated by the place of the chapter within the plan and by the subject matter. The speeches in III.14 are addressed directly or indirectly to people who were more or less incontinent in regard to food. The concluding theme of the Book may therefore be said to be continence. We remember the importance which that theme had—second only to piety—in the beginning of this part of the *Memorabilia* (I.3–III.14). The addressees in this chapter were men who "dined together" with Socrates: they were not men who simply "were together" with him, i.e., his companions. One of the speeches reported here was about "names," i.e., words: there is nowhere here a speech dealing with any "what is." The occasion was that one of those present ate the meat "itself by itself," i.e., without bread. In accordance with this the last speech of the Book deals with Socrates' interpretation of a term used "in the tongue of the Athenians."

Book IV

The bulk of the *Memorabilia* (I.3–IV) consists of two parts: I.3–III and IV. Just as III.14 is an unparalleled end, IV.1 is an unparalleled beginning.

Since IV is the last Book, its last chapter is the end both of IV and of the whole work. That chapter is reasonably devoted to the end of Socrates and Xenophon's eulogy of him. IV begins with an introduction (chapter 1) that is an introduction only to IV.

IV.1 In that introduction Xenophon first draws this conclusion from the preceding part, i.e., from I.3–III: Socrates was most useful to his companions in every thing and in every manner or in every place and in every thing. In each chapter of the preceding part Xenophon had shown that Socrates was most useful to his companions in this or that manner, in this or that thing, in this or that place (e.g., in the workshop of Pistias or in the dwelling of Theodote), although the "thing" and the "place" were made clearer than the "manner." After having risen from the particulars to the general, he makes three further remarks. (1) Even remembering Socrates when he was absent was of no small benefit to those who were accustomed to be with him and who accepted what he thought: writing his *Recollections* was of no small benefit to Xenophon. (2) Socrates was helpful to his companions not only when he was serious but also when he was joking: speaking jocularly is a kind of being absent, namely from those who do not understand that what is said is not seriously or literally meant. For instance, Socrates often said that he was in love with someone. Yet he manifestly did not desire those distinguished by the bloom of their beautiful bodies but those who were by nature fit for virtue of the soul. The latter—those possessing or being "good natures"—are those who learn quickly whatever they apply themselves to, remember what they have learned, and have a desire for all branches of knowledge by means of which one can nobly inhabit a house as well as a city and in general make a good use of human beings and of human things. Men of this kind, Socrates thought, would, if educated, not only be happy themselves and nobly manage their households but could

also make other men and cities happy. Xenophon makes here
no reservation to the effect that the good education of the good
natures is successful only if chance or the gods do not inter-
vene. There is some ambiguity here as to whether the knowledge desired by the good natures aims at the best state of a
radically private life or whether it aims in the first place at
the management of the households and secondarily at the management of cities. Perhaps one can say that the natural desire
of good natures is directed toward the former whereas that
desire if molded by education is directed toward the latter. Be
this as it may, Xenophon's central remark here compels us to
consider whether all interlocutors of Socrates who were presented in the preceding Books were good natures and which,
if any, were not: we easily could have read those Books without wondering at all whether the interlocutors presented there
were good natures. The distinction between the natures that
are good and those that are not is not unrelated to the distinction between the good friends of Socrates and those who were
his friends in a loose sense of the word. (3) Socrates approached
different kinds of people in different manners. This may be
said to be implied in the second remark, given the fact that he
conversed not only with men or youths with whom he was in
love. Xenophon gives here two examples of the different manners in which Socrates approached different kinds of people:
those who believe they are by nature good but despise learning
or education, and those who are proud of their wealth and do
not believe that they need any education in addition to their
wealth. He approached the former by granting to them that
they were most well-born, as they believed or were thought to
be, and by showing them that precisely if this were true they
were in special need of education and learning; they may be
good natures in the sense that they learn quickly and remember

what they have learned, but they are not good natures simply since they have no desire for all branches of the knowledge in question. He approached the latter by showing that men of their kind are foolish and senseless. Both kinds of men are not good natures since they do not have a spontaneous desire for learning the most important things.

In the second chapter Xenophon shows how Socrates approached a third kind of man, namely, he who holds that he is in possession of the best education and thinks highly of his wisdom. But in this case he shows at considerable length how Socrates approached an individual of this species, the fair (and young) Euthydemos. Euthydemos had collected many writings of the most renowned poets as well as sophists; he held that he therefore surpassed in wisdom his contemporaries and had great hopes that he could surpass all others in power of speaking and acting. Being a youth of this kind, Euthydemos had no longer a desire for learning and had had at all times a rather perverse desire for learning: he was not a good nature. Xenophon is silent on how Socrates approached the good natures: almost all conversations in IV are with Euthydemos, with one and the same interlocutor. This is another striking difference between IV and I.3–III. Furthermore, in Book IV there is no discussion of the subjects "relatives," "friends," and "men desiring the noble things"; only "the man himself" is discussed.

Finally, IV differs strikingly from I.3–III since the bulk of IV (chapters 2–7) presents the core of Socrates' teaching according to its intrinsic order from its beginning to its end. Those chapters partly "repeat" the subjects of earlier chapters but they treat these subjects from a new point of view and according to a new plan. For instance, IV.3 repeats I.4; these chapters are the only ones devoted to Socratic conversations about the gods; yet the first of these two conversations owes its place to Xenophon's still following the "plan" of Socrates' indictment, whereas the second owes its place to the order of Socrates' teaching.

The bulk of IV presents the core of Socrates' teaching according to its intrinsic order with a view to the capacity or the needs of "Euthydemos." This assertion seems to be incompatible with the fact that IV.4 transmits a Socratic conversation, not with Euthydemos, but with the sophist Hippias. We shall take up this difficulty in the proper place.

IV.2. In order to urge Euthydemos toward learning, Socrates had to convince him of his ignorance. To achieve this he had some conversations in his presence; all took place appropriately in a bridle maker's shop. In the first conversation Socrates replied to the question raised by someone as to whether Themistokles owed his rank in the city to his intercourse with some wise man or to his nature; since Themistokles owed his rank solely to his nature (Thucydides, I.137.3), Socrates gave only the general reply that it would be silly to believe that one could become a first rate statesman without having had an adequate teacher; Socrates gave this reply "with a view to" Euthydemos. In the second conversation Socrates openly and effectively ridiculed Euthydemos for his silly belief that he could become an outstanding Athenian without having had any teacher and for his still sillier concern with appearing never to have had a teacher. He stressed the fact that the need for teachers is greatest in the case of those who wish to excel in statesmanship. Since Euthydemos was anxious not to appear to admire Socrates' wisdom, Socrates could not talk to him but only about him. By publicly ridiculing Euthydemos for his silliness Socrates caught his attention and made an impression on him. He began to listen to Socrates yet he still kept aloof in order to appear to be superior. Thereupon Socrates changed his approach and ceased to ridicule him; he tried to build him a golden bridge; he reasserted in a quite inoffensive manner what he had asserted earlier in a manner which could offend. When he noticed that Euthydemos had become rather willing to listen to what he said, he went the next time to the bridle maker's shop alone and engaged Euthydemos in a private conversation. Euthydemos was unable to explain why he had collected and was still collecting many writings of men said to be wise. Socrates extracted from him successively the replies that he did not collect his treasures in order to become a good physician, architect, geometer, astronomer, or rhapsode; the central question concerned geometry: it is the only question in which Socrates mentions an outstanding practitioner (Theodoros). Only in the case of the rhapsodes did Euthydemos give a reason: Homer's works are a most important, if not the most important, part of his library. Finally when he asked him whether he longs for that virtue on account of which human beings become able to manage households and cities, fit to rule and useful to the other human beings as well as to themselves, Euthydemos gave an affirmative reply in a most lively manner. Socrates praised him for longing for the most noble virtue and the greatest art, which is justly called the kingly art.

However confused Euthydemos may have been concerning the virtue or art he longed for, he had given thought to the fact that one cannot be a good citizen—let alone a good ruler—without being just. He is quite sure that he himself is just and that he knows what being just means. Socrates proposes that they should write down a *J* and an *I* and subsume under either letter the acts of justice and injustice respectively. Euthydemos does not see why this is at all needed but he has no objection to Socrates' doing the writing. The proposal and its execution are remarkable since Socrates as a rule did not write.

Replying to Socrates' questions Euthydemos decides that lying, deceiving, mistreating, and selling free men into slavery clearly fall under injustice. Thereupon Socrates brings Euthydemos to admit that the enslaving of the citizens of an unjust and hostile city and deceiving, stealing, and robbing, if done in war, are just. It thus becomes clear that the actions in question are unjust only if done to friends (fellow citizens and allies). (It is no longer said that they are just only if done to unjust enemies.) Yet if a general lies to his discouraged soldiers and deceives them in order to encourage them, or a father deceives his son in order to make him swallow a medicine, or if one steals from a depressed friend something with which he might kill himself or takes it away from him by force, he acts justly. Socrates tacitly suggests that according to Euthydemos, justice consists in helping one's friends (and hurting the enemies) rather than in refraining from the particular actions enumerated. When Socrates raises the further question as to who is more unjust, he who deliberately acts unjustly or he who does it involuntarily, Euthydemos confesses that he had lost his confidence in his answers; but Socrates forces him to admit that contrary to his opinion the former is less unjust than the latter, just as he who deliberately errs in writing or reading, i.e., who knows the letters properly, is more literate than he who errs in this respect involuntarily: he who knows the just things is juster than he who does not know them. Euthydemos thus comes to realize that he, who believed he had been philosophizing in the right manner, does not know what he believed to know, namely, the noble, the good, and the just things and hence that he has the disposition of a slave. He is utterly discouraged; he does not see any other way to gentlemanship except the one which led him into utter ignorance.

Socrates asks him whether he had ever taken the way to

Delphi and noticed at the temple there the inscription "Know thyself." He had, even twice, but he had not given it any thought since he believed to know himself thoroughly: self-knowledge is easier to obtain than any other knowledge (for instance, the art of farming). We see from this example how he had read the many writings that he had collected. Socrates makes clear to him that through self-knowledge, through men's knowledge of what they need and what they are able to procure, they acquire the good things and guard against the bad ones; through their knowledge of those things and their ensuing success they become famed and honored and are desired by others as protectors, nay, rulers. He makes here a clear, if tacit, distinction between the good things and the noble ones; the former are more fundamental than the latter. It follows that one cannot know oneself—one's worth or lack of it—if one does not know what sorts of things are good and what sorts are bad.

Euthydemos does not have the slightest doubt that he knows these things. He is as certain that he knows them as he was certain that he knows the just things and that he knows himself. He is certain in the first place that being healthy and what causes health are good and sickness and what causes sickness are bad. But Socrates draws his attention to the fact that both health and sickness are good if they are responsible for something good and bad if they are responsible for something bad. For instance, health may be the cause of a man's taking part in a disgraceful military expedition and thus perishing while the opposite would be true of sickness (cf. Aristotle, *Nicomachean Ethics* 1094b16–19). Generally speaking, since "the good things" are sometimes helpful but sometimes harmful it seems to be wrong to call them good. Yet whatever may be true of other things thought to be good, Euthydemos asserts that wisdom at any rate is indisputably good. He does not say that justice is indisputably good (cf. *Symposium* 3.4) because he had come to see how disputable justice is. Socrates proves to him through two mythical and an indefinite number of barbarian examples of men who were enslaved or perished because of their wisdom, that wisdom is by no means always good; the central example is that of Palamedes, who perished because he was envied on account of his wisdom. (That Socrates perished could be traced to the fact that he was envied on account of his wisdom—*Education of Cyrus* III.1.38–39). Euthydemos had perhaps never heard of the wise men who were kidnapped so that they would be slaves of the king of Persia; the two mythical examples suffice for convincing him of his error. He draws the conclusion that the least disputable good is being happy. Yet happiness would not be indisputably good if it were not possible without such things as beauty, strength, wealth, and reputation, i.e., without disputable goods; for these things may be as ruinous as wisdom. Socrates seems to admit that happiness is indisputably good precisely because, in contradistinction to Euthydemos, he does not regard the ambiguous things mentioned as conditions or ingredients of happiness. But if even his praise of happiness is wrong, Euthydemos exclaims, he must admit that he does not know for what to pray to the gods. It does not occur to him that he could pray to the all-knowing gods to give him what they know to be unambiguously good for him (I.3.3). Or can even the gods not give things which are unambiguously good? Euthydemos' ignorance of the good and bad things prevents him from knowing what democracy is, although he is eager to become a leader in a democracy. He holds that the ruler in a democracy, the *demos*, is the poor and that he knows the poor as well as the rich: the poor are those who do not have enough to pay for what they want, while the rich are those who have more than enough. Yet, as Socrates reminds him, some who possess very little can even make savings out of it, while for others who have very much their wealth is not sufficient; those so-called rich would be poor and vice versa. Euthydemos remembers now in particular the straits in which some tyrants find themselves: the tyrants belong to the *demos* and the poor who manage their little property well, to the rich. But if the tyrant belongs to the *demos,* is the rule of tyrants not democracy? Or is democracy tyrannical? Does this perhaps follow directly from the difficulties regarding justice, regarding law, of which we have heard earlier (I.2.40–45)? Euthydemos is compelled to admit that tyrants belong to the *demos;* he traces that compulsion however not to the truth of what he had admitted but to the inferioriy of his understanding.

Thus he went away utterly disheartened and filled with self-contempt. At the same time he realized that he could in no other way become a remarkable man except by being together with Socrates as much as circumstances would permit. Apart from being together with Socrates, he even imitated some of his pursuits. Socrates naturally no longer disheartened and perplexed him but explained in the simplest and least obscure manner what in his opinion one should know and one should preferably practice. Many others were as much discouraged by Socrates as Euthydemos, yet they therefore never came back to him. Socrates regarded them as rather negligent (cf. *Oeconomicus* VIII.16). We have to add here this remark: the fact that Euthydemos was a better man than those who avoided Socrates because he had deflated them does not prove that he was a good nature. Since even good natures are at least primarily under the spell of unexamined opinions regarding the most important things, we assume that Socrates applied his elenctic art to the good natures as well.

The chapter under discussion deals successively with these three subjects: the just things, self-knowledge, and the good things. This implies that the just things are not the same as the good things; all just things may be good, but the inverse is not true. Hence it is possible that all four Socratic writings present Socrates' goodness (virtue) but only the *Memorabilia* presents his justice.

IV.3. Xenophon introduces his account of the core of Socrates' nonelenctic teaching as presented to Euthydemos with these words: "He did not hasten his companions' becoming skilled in speaking, in doing, and in devising [or contriving or deliberating; cf. the tripartition here with that in I.1.19; for the meaning of *mechanikos* see especially *Hellenica* III.1.8]. But he believed that prior to these powers moderation [*sophrosyne*] ought to emerge in them; for he held that those who possess these powers without being moderate would be more unjust and have greater power for mischief [than otherwise]. In the first place therefore he tried to make his companions moderate as regards the gods." As is implied here and becomes clearer from the two subsequent chapters, the other part of moderation is moderation as regards human beings, i.e., justice. Moderation thus understood is a prerequisite for becoming a Socratic expert in speaking, doing, and silently deliberating (cf. I.2.17). Moderation in this sense is not the same as temperance; the opposite of moderation in our sense is not intemperance but *hybris* (cf. I.1.16 and I.2.19).

Considering the importance of the subject it is not surprising that Socrates conversed on it with quite a few individuals and that ear-witnesses reported these conversations. Xenophon, who was present at his conversations on this subject with Eu-thydemos, gives a report which does not claim to be quite literal. It may seem strange that Xenophon here as it were forgets his own earlier narrative of Socrates' conversation about the gods with Aristodemos—a conversation at which he was also present (I.4). Yet that conversation had an entirely different meaning or purport than the present one. The con-versation with Euthydemos, to repeat, is meant to be the first section of Socrates' regular nonelenctic teaching as conveyed to Euthydemos and with a view to Euthydemos; the conversa-tion with Aristodemos however shows how Socrates assisted him at a moment of urgent need. Aristodemos, who was nick-named "the Small," not only did not sacrifice to the gods and make use of divination but even ridiculed those who acted cor-rectly in these matters; we may say that he was a contradictor in deed. The beautiful Euthydemos however was not doing or saying anything unbecoming. Xenophon surely says nothing to the effect that he did not sacrifice and the like.

Euthydemos, as he admits frankly, had not given any thought to the care with which the gods supply men's wants. Aris-todemos on the other hand had broken with the customary practices precisely because he had given thought, if deplorably insufficient thought, to that care: he thought that the gods do not care at all for men.

The argument addressed to Euthydemos starts from our need for light and moves from there to the benefits that the gods bestow upon us through the sun, the stars, and the moon as well as earth, water, and fire. (This whole argument has no parallel in the conversation with Aristodemos.) We need fire in particular as a help against cold and darkness, a help which the sun and the moon apparently do not always provide; yet fire too is a gift of the gods. Whether Socrates thus rejects or modifies the myth of Prometheus' theft of fire must be left open. We should note however his silence on the fourth element: "air" occurs in Xenophon only in the compound "measuring the air," an activity which is comically ascribed to Socrates (*Oeconomicus* XI.3; cf. the reading of N in IV.3.7).

Furthermore, Aristodemos is convinced by Socrates' questions that the god is an artificer who loves animals in general while indeed taking special care of men. Euthydemos however is led by Socrates' questions to wonder whether the gods do anything but serve human beings; what prevents him from regarding the gods as being nothing but philanthropic is the fact that they care also for the other animals; Socrates shows him therefore that the animals other than man live only for man's sake; this extremely anthropocentric thought, namely that the other animals, just like the heavenly bodies and the elements, exist only for the sake of man, is absent from the conversation with Aristodemos. Yet when proving to Euthydemos that the other animals exist only for the sake of men, Socrates limits himself to speaking of the domestic or useful animals.

Besides, when Socrates comes to speak to Euthydemos about the peculiar benefits which the gods have bestowed upon man, i.e., about human nature, he is silent about the peculiarities of the human body (erect posture, hands, and tongue) of which he had spoken to Aristodemos; on the other hand, he is somewhat more explicit about the peculiarities of the human soul in speaking to Euthydemos than in speaking to Aristodemos; in particular he mentions law-making among the benefits due to speech whereas he had mentioned to Aristodemos the awareness of the existence of the gods, who have put together in order the greatest and most beautiful things, i.e., the *kosmos*, as a most noble peculiarity of man's soul.

In addition, Aristodemos is not persuaded by Socrates that the gods are concerned with Aristodemos; to convince him, the gods would have to send counselors as to how he should act, as Socrates indeed asserts that the gods do; Socrates' assertion does not remove Aristodemos' doubt. Socrates tries to convince him by reminding him of the well-known fact of divination; Aristodemos remains silent. When speaking to Euthydemos however Socrates mentions divination spontaneously as a further sign of the gods' special care for man; Euthydemos refers to Socrates' *daimonion* (without using the term) as a sign that Socrates is still more favored by the gods than other men. Whether Euthydemos has doubts regarding divination in general and the divination peculiar to Socrates in particular is, to say the least, less clear than that Aristodemos has such doubts. At any rate Socrates proves to him the truth of divination and of his *daimonion*, or of his theology and the need for piety as a whole by this consideration: he must not wait until he sees the shapes of the gods but must be content with seeing the gods' works. The gods themselves intimate this. The other gods when giving us good things and the god who orders and keeps together the whole *kosmos*, in which everything is good and fine (cf. II.2.3), both become visible in or through their works. Furthermore, the sun does not permit human beings to observe it carefully but if someone tries to behold it shamelessly, it takes away his sight. Exact observation and reverence seem to be incompatible. Also the ministers of the gods like thunderbolts and winds are invisible. To say nothing of lightning, is the sun only a minister of the gods or is he himself a god? What Socrates says to Euthydemos could suggest that he did not regard the sun as a god (cf. Plato, *Apol. Socr.* 26c7–d5; cf. *Memorabilia* IV.7.7). Above all, if any other human thing participates in the divine, the human soul does, and the human soul is not visible while its work in us is manifest. Aristodemos had used the invisibility of the gods as an argument for supporting the doubt in their existence and in refuting that argument Socrates had not spoken of the invisibility (or quasi-invisibility) of the sun, lightning, and winds.

Euthydemos is disheartened because he does not see how any man could ever render proper thanks to the gods. Socrates comforts him by reminding him of the answer which the god in Delphi gives when someone asks him how he could gratify the gods: by obeying the law of the city, for it is presumably everywhere the law that one pleases the gods with sacrifices according to his power. In talking to Euthydemos Socrates does not trace this maxim to Hesiod (I.3.3) nor indeed to the Delphic god. For how can one please the gods more than by obeying them to the highest degree? Since Aristodemos did not experience Euthydemos' discouragement, he did not receive the comfort which Socrates gives to Euthydemos. The reference to the Delphic god is noteworthy since the arguments established only the existence of what we may call the cosmic gods. The reference to the Delphic god who refers the questioners to the law of the city as well as the previous mention of law-making has no parallel in the conversation with Aristodemos; they suitably prepare the argument of the next chapter.

By saying things of this kind and himself doing them Socrates made his companions more pious as well as more moderate: piety and moderation are two different things and not merely because moderation comprises justice as well as piety.

IV.4. This chapter, devoted to justice as the other part of moderation, differs from the other chapters of the group to which it belongs because it opens with a rather extensive account of Socrates' deed as distinguished from his speech. No comparable account is given in the preceding chapter of Soc-

rates' piety in deed or in the subsequent chapter of his continence in deed. The reason is obvious: Socrates' being pious
and continent in deed had been shown in the refutation of the
indictment and in the subsequent chapter (I.1–3). But this
observation leads only to these two further questions. (1) Must
one not always be mindful of the fact that IV is situated, or
moves, on a different plane than I–III? What may have been
adequate for the purposes of the first three Books is perhaps
no longer adequate on the new plane. From what Socrates said
to Euthydemos about piety we might learn that a man who
obeys the law of the city as regards the actions of honoring the
gods is pious. If justice should prove to be the same as obeying
the laws of the city, one might therefore say, if one wishes, that
piety is a part of justice; by proving that Socrates obeyed the
laws of the city one would prove that he was pious. (2) Why
does Xenophon present Socrates' being just in deed in IV.4
only? To this question one could reply that the whole *Memorabilia* is devoted to showing Socrates' justice in deed. Yet
justice as meant in this true statement is either too narrow or
too broad; for it means either that he was not guilty of the two
particular crimes of which he was accused in the indictment or
that he never harmed anyone in any way but helped those who
made use of him in the greatest things; but as we have learned
from the elenctic conversation with Euthydemos, harming the
enemies of the city is part of justice.

According to the account given in the sole chapter explicitly
devoted to justice—the central conversation in Book IV—
Socrates was just because he was eminently law-abiding; *nomos*
and derivatives occur in this account with unusual frequency.
Xenophon had spoken of Socrates' law-abidingness at the end
of his refutation of the indictment (I.2.62–63): he did not steal,
cut purses, rob temples, and the like; Xenophon seems here to

imply that actions like corrupting the young—to say nothing of impious actions—are not, or should not be, forbidden by the law.

Xenophon states first in general that Socrates showed his justice both in private life by behaving lawfully as well as helpfully toward all, and in public life by obeying the lawful commands of the rulers both at home and on campaigns: public life does not permit one's being helpful, to all, especially to the public enemies; and acting lawfully is not the same as acting helpfully. Xenophon then gives three instances of Socrates' just, i.e., law-abiding conduct in public life: his conduct at the trial of the generals who were in command at the battle of Arginusai, his conduct under the rule of the Thirty, and his conduct at his trial when he was accused by Meletos. Each of the first two instances had been mentioned once before. It is instructive to compare the two versions. In the first version of the first instance Socrates' impressive conduct was adduced as the strongest proof of his piety, for by refusing to act against the law on this occasion he refused to commit perjury (I.1.17–18). In the first version of the second instance Socrates' conduct was not presented as a proof of his justice or law-abidingness; on the contrary, according to the first version Socrates did not question Kritias' being a law-giver and he was perfectly willing to obey Kritias' law which forbade him to converse with the young, i.e., to teach them the art of speaking (I.2.31 ff.). It is not sufficient to say that Socrates' recognizing Kritias' authority when he talked to him was ironical; for one must show first that he regarded the laws of democratic Athens as sacrosanct or, generally stated, that he was unaware of the fact that laws are relative to the regime. As for the third instance, Xenophon traces Socrates' conduct at his trial in the repetition (IV.8.5–8) not to his law-abidingness but to his *daimonion* or the god's view that it was time for Socrates to die.

Socrates spoke frequently to various men in praise of law-abidingness. Xenophon reports, again not quite literally, his conversation on justice with Hippias of Elis. (The conversation with Hippias is the central conversation in IV.2–6 just as the conversation with Antiphon is the central conversation in I.4–II.1; these two conversations are the only ones with sophists. The symmetry—the conversation with a sophist surrounded on each side by two conversations with nonsophists—is, as one could expect, more visible in IV.2–6 than in I.4–II.1.) Why did he not report a Socratic conversation on justice with Euthydemos? Hippias was famous or notorious as a despiser of the laws; proving to Hippias that the just is the legal is a much greater feat and has a much more persuasive power than proving it to Euthydemos. (Let no one say that by parity of reasoning Socrates ought to have conversed on piety with a despiser of piety; for he had conversed on piety with Aristodemos.) This does not mean that he thus deprived Euthydemos of this important instruction, for it is by no means impossible that Euthydemos was present at the conversation with Hippias. We do not say that Euthydemos was prepared for this conversation, since he may have read writings of Hippias; for we never heard that he read the writings of the most famous sophists; we only heard that he collected those writings (IV.2.1 and IV.2.8). Euthydemos was prepared for Socrates' conversation with Hippias as a result of the elenctic conversation. There Euthydemos had learned that he is completely ignorant as regards justice. One might say that that conversation had led to a positive, if implicit, result: justice consists in helping one's friends and harming one's enemies. But this result is clearly insufficient; to say nothing of other considerations, it is silent on the fact that one has greater obligations to one's parents than to one's friends. This difficulty at any rate is overcome by the view that the just is the same as the legal (II.2.13). Be this as it may, we must be thankful to Xenophon that his Euthydemos did not answer in the elenctic conversation that the just is the legal. No doubt, Socrates, who could use any interlocutor in what manner he wished (I.2.14), could have refuted that definition. But would he have been able to restore it to Euthydemos' satisfaction? Yet by proving it to Hippias, he established it in Euthydemos' mind forever.

After Hippias had been absent from Athens for some time, he came on Socrates, who said to some men that amazingly it is easy to find teachers of the various arts while if someone wants to learn the just one does not know where to turn. This is a strange introduction to a conversation in which Socrates proves that the just is the legal, for there are always and everywhere many who can teach the law. Hippias is amused that Socrates still says the same things which he said when Hippias was at Athens quite some time ago. Socrates contends that he always says the same things about the same subjects, whereas Hippias because of his extensive learning never says the same things about the same subject: he always tries to say something new. When questioned by Socrates he admits that he always says the same things whenever he is asked how many and which are the letters in "Socrates"—knowledge of one's name is a kind of self-knowledge which everyone possesses (cf. IV.2.24) —and whether two times five are ten but the case of justice is obviously different; yet he has now an irrefutable (and of course entirely new) speech on justice. Socrates is greatly pleased by the prospect that henceforth jurymen will cease to give conflicting votes, citizens will cease to contradict one another regarding the just things, to litigate, and to start revolts, and cities will cease to disagree about the just things and go to war. In the context of the chapter this means that even if the just is the same as the legal, the confusion referred to will not cease, and we still would have to wish for men who know not merely the legal but the just as well. Hippias claims to know the just. Socrates is eager to hear his speech on justice but Hippias refuses to do Socrates the favor: Socrates will hear Hippias' speech only after he has said what he holds justice to be, for he never says what he thinks on any subject but ridicules others by questioning those who make assertions and refuting them. Accordingly we do not hear Hippias' speech, which surely was not to the effect that the just is the same as the legal, just as we never hear through Xenophon any sophist's speech about piety and the gods. To Hippias' remark, which someone might find somewhat insulting, Socrates replies that he constantly reveals his opinion on the just things by deed, which is a more trustworthy revelation than by speech; he never bears false witness or does any other unjust thing; the answer does not satisfy Hippias although Socrates thinks that unwillingness to do injustice is a sufficient display of justice. (Unwillingnesss to do injustice is not the same as never committing an unjust act. One may commit an unjust act without intending it; on the other hand, one's intention may always remain a mere intention if there are no occasions for acting unjustly or temptations to act unjustly; cf. *Education of Cyrus* V.2.9.) Socrates proves to Hippias now that the legal (lawful, law-abiding) is just; Hippias understands this to mean that the legal and the just are the same, and Socrates accepts this interpretation. Socrates might have meant that everything legal is just but not everything just is legal (prescribed by law). (Cf. the distinction between the legal and the useful in IV.4.1 with the definition of justice implied in IV.8.11.) Since Hippias does not understand which sort

of legal and which sort of just Socrates means, Socrates explains
to him that in speaking of the legal he has in mind the laws of
the city. According to Hippias the laws of the city are coven-
ants made by the citizens as to what should be done and for-
borne. Since he speaks of the citizens and not of the multitude
(I.2.42), his definition of law covers all republican laws but
not the royal laws. Hippias objects to Socrates' identification of
the just with the legal on the ground that one cannot take the
laws seriously, seeing that the men who pass them frequently
repeal them. This causes no difficulty according to Socrates
since the cities also frequently undertake a war and then make
peace; therefore if Hippias disparages those who obey the laws
on the ground that those laws may be repealed, he must also
censure those who keep discipline in war on the ground that
there will again be peace; or does Hippias censure also those
who in wars eagerly help their fatherlands? However much of a
wandering sophist he may be, Hippias cannot resist this appeal
to his civic or patriotic feeling. Socrates strengthens his appeal
still more by reminding him of the fact that Sparta is so superior to the other cities because it is singularly law-abiding.
Moreover, in all cities concord (*homonoia*) is regarded as a
very great good, but what else does this mean except that the
citizens ought to be of one mind in regard to obeying the laws?
He then speaks copiously of the great benefits which accrue
to the law-abiding man. Socrates draws the conclusion that the
same is legal and just. Swearing by Zeus, Hippias agrees.

Needless to say that by having pointed out the great virtue
of law-abidingness Socrates has not proved that the legal and
the just are the same. This explains why he now abruptly turns
to the unwritten laws. According to Hippias the unwritten laws
obtain in every country in the same sense and have been laid
down by gods; accordingly, all men regard it as a law in the

first place to worship gods. (This does not conflict with Socrates' or Apollon's view that one ought to sacrifice to the gods according to the laws of the city; for while the gods demand that men sacrifice to them, one city demands that on a given occasion one sacrifice a goat and another city that one sacrifice a sheep; cf. Aristotle, *Eth. Nic.* 1134b19–22). Hippias replies in the affirmative to Socrates' question whether honoring one's parents is also regarded everywhere as a law. But he replies in the negative to Socrates' question whether the prohibition against incest between parents and children or between children and parents belongs to the same class of laws, for, he says, he sees that some transgress that law. He obviously implies that unwritten laws are never transgressed and in particular that the laws enjoining honoring the gods and the parents are never transgressed by anyone; whether he thinks so from innocence or from the lack of it, we are in no position to tell. Socrates however holds that a law is unwritten or divine, not because it is never transgressed, but because its transgressors cannot possibly escape punishment, as one can escape punishment for transgressing any human law. According to this view, men who transgress the two laws which Hippias declared to be divine—honoring gods and parents—would not escape punishment even if they escaped human justice. But this is not what Socrates says about these two laws; he does not assert that, nor show how, not worshipping the gods carries with it its own punishment; perhaps he thought that in these cases punishment does not automatically follow the transgression but is inflicted on the transgressor by men or gods. In the case of incest between parents and children however the automatic punishment consists in the defective character of the offspring, for good offspring can come only from parents who are both in their prime. Socrates suggests in other words that divine punishment (and reward) is the same as the natural consequence of a human action. Hippias agrees to what Socrates says. This does not mean that he is wise in agreeing. It is unnecessary to mention the fact that the Socratic argument is silent about incest between brother and sister. The Socratic argument implies that the punishment for incest between parents and children does not differ from the "punishment" that is visited on any oldish husband who married a young wife (Hugo Grotius, *De jure belli ac pacis* II.5.12, 4). Socrates finally shows that the law forbidding ingratitude is likewise divine in his sense. In conclusion he asks Hippias whether he thinks that the gods legislate the just things or other things. Hippias replies that if a god does not legislate the just things, hardly anyone else would. Socrates infers from this that it pleases the gods too that the same is just as well as legal. Hippias does not contradict him. We on our part conclude that Hippias' final statement implies a recognition of the fact that the just things are as such different from the legal. (Cf. I.2.9–11.)

The inadequacy of Socrates' proof stands in a superficial contrast to the fact that the conversation with Hippias and the whole group of conversations to which it belongs are meant to present the Socratic teaching according to its intrinsic order. Yet that teaching is in the main presented with a view to Euthydemos. We see now that the situation is not greatly altered if Hippias takes Euthydemos' place.

According to Xenophon's final sentence, by saying as well as doing things of this kind Socrates made those who approached him more just. He does not say that Socrates made them more law-abiding. Socrates surely made Hippias aware that disparaging the laws on the ground which he adduced is tantamount to disparaging patriotic war efforts. Above all, he made him aware of his place. At the beginning Hippias refused to answer Socratic questions in order not to undergo the humiliation of being refuted and thus becoming ridiculous; yet in the whole exchange regarding the just and the legal he is forced by Socrates into the role of the respondent who only rarely raises objections, and of these objections Socrates disposes with ease. Being made aware of the superiority of a man whom one regards as one's inferior or equal means however being made more just. Besides, while the identification of the just with the legal is theoretically wrong, it is practically as a rule correct.

IV.5. Socrates enabled his companions to become skilled in doing by increasing their continence. His educating human beings in or to continence had been discussed in the first section of the bulk of the work, especially in his nondialogic exhortation to continence (I.5). We recall two points that are important for the understanding of his conversation with Euthydemos on the subject. According to the earlier statement, continence is compatible with greed, one of the roots of injustice, and continence is the foundation of virtue: it is the foundation of virtue and not a virtue because it can also be the foundation of certain vices. In the Euthydemean context the education to continence is preceded by training in moderation (piety and justice); a man thus trained is no longer in danger of being or becoming greedy; hence Socrates is now silent on the possible abuse of continence. Continence, control over the pleasures enjoyed by means of the body, is useful, i.e., the foundation, for these good things or virtues: freedom of both the individual and the city, wisdom, and moderation. Freedom means here the ability to do what is best or most noble. Wisdom is here asserted by Socrates to be the greatest good. It is the only statement ever made by Socrates on what is the greatest good. He does not give Euthydemos an opportunity to agree or disagree with this assertion; his present assertion does not contradict what he had urged earlier against Euthydemos (IV.2.23): for wisdom may very well be the greatest good without being good for all human beings in all circumstances; continence, on the other hand, seems to be best for a human being: it is not the greatest good: continence will then be in the best case the foundation for wisdom. Moderation differs from wisdom as caring, practice, assiduity differ from knowledge. The silence here on piety and justice does not require further explanation. Socrates draws Euthydemos' attention next to the paradoxical fact that the continent man who always prefers the good to the pleasant is the only one to derive an enjoyment worth remembering and worth mentioning from the bodily pleasures and to enjoy the very great pleasures following virtuous activity. Only the continent can contemplate the most excellent things and sort out (*dialegein*)—the most excellent things? or the good and bad things?—by deed and by speech (cf. *Oeconomicus* VIII.9 and 19–20, also IX.6–8) and thus choose the good things and abstain from the bad ones. By acting thus men will become not only best as well as most happy but also most capable of conversing (*dialegesthai*). According to Socrates *dialegesthai* has received its name from men's coming together in order to deliberate jointly by sorting things out (*dialegein*) according to classes. Through doing this to the highest degree, men become best as well as most capable of leadership and most able to converse (*dialektikotatoi*). Continence that makes men experts in doing is the foundation above all for dialectical skill, a fact not mentioned in the earlier discussions of continence. The relation of dialectical skill to the greatest good, wisdom, is left in the dark for the time being.

As Xenophon intimates, at the end of this chapter, the happiest of men are those who are most fit for leadership. For the chapter deals with how Socrates made his companions skilled in doing. It is the function of the leader to make happy those whom he leads (III.2) but he is happier than all of them, just as Socrates was more blessed than his followers.

IV.6. Xenophon will now say how Socrates increased his companions' conversational or dialectical skill. He had originally mentioned Socrates' increasing his companions' skill in speaking (IV.3.1). Does he mean now that he will not speak of Socrates as teacher of rhetoric? The *Memorabilia* as a whole seems to call for an affirmative answer. Apart from Xenophon's narrative the work consists almost exclusively of Socratic conversations; the only exceptions are Socrates' nondialogic speeches (I.5, I.7, II.4; cf. also II.1.21–33 and *Oeconomicus* V.1–17, XX.2–24, and XXI.2–12). Or is the art of speaking as practiced and taught by Socrates identical with his conversational art? (Cf. I.7, end, and IV.4.4) This is surely one of the difficulties that induce Xenophon to say here—what he does not say elsewhere—that he will "try" to deal with the subject of the chapter. (Xenophon also does not speak here, as he did when introducing the conversation on continence, of "all companions"—IV.5.2.)

Socrates held that those who know "what each of the beings is" are also able to expound this knowledge to others, while it is not surprising that those who do not know, err themselves and lead others into error. "Therefore he never ceased considering together with his companions what each of the beings is." This statement seems to be at variance with the bulk of the *Memorabilia*. Which "what is" question does Socrates raise for instance when he gives advice to Aristarchos (cf. II.7.3), who is ruined by his female relatives, or to Kriton, who is annoyed by the sycophants? Perhaps Socrates never ceased considering what each of the beings is silently "in the midst of his companions" (the reading of B), even if he did not consider it "together with his companions." One could also say that Xenophon here points to the center of Socrates' life—a center of which he does not speak owing to the limitation he has imposed on himself especially in the *Memorabilia*.

Xenophon no longer says as he had said near the beginning of the work (I.1.16) that Socrates raised the "what is" questions regarding the human things only. The simple exclusion of the nonhuman things would hardly be feasible after Xenophon had spoken of Socrates' use of observations regarding the sun in his demonstration of the existence of gods (IV.3).

The speeches that resemble most the ones transmitted in the chapter devoted to Socrates as a teacher of the dialectical art are the speeches transmitted in III.8–9. But in III.8–9 nothing is said about dialectics and about wisdom as distinguished from the other virtues being the greatest good, and we find there only two explicit "what is" questions. In other words, IV.6 is the peak of Book IV, whereas III.8–9 marks the beginning of the descent. On the other hand, whereas the interlocutor in IV.6 is Euthydemos, the interlocutor in III.8.1–7 is the philosopher Aristippos; it is unknown to whom Socrates talks in the rest of III.8–9.

Since Socrates considered what each of the beings is, Xenophon cannot well present the results of these considerations without defeating the purpose of the *Memorabilia*. He will therefore give only as many specimens as in his opinion will make manifest the manner of Socrates' inquiry. The first specimen is of course the inquiry as to what piety is (cf. I.1.16 and IV.3). There is no parallel to this inquiry in III.8–9. Euthydemos regards piety as something very fine and he understands by a pious man one who honors the gods according to the laws according to which one ought to honor them. Socrates draws from this the conclusion, accepted by Euthydemos, that a man who knows the laws in question would know how one ought to honor the gods and, since no one honors the gods except in the manner in which he believes that one ought to honor them, that the pious man is he who knows what is lawful regarding the gods. We note that the pious man knows the laws in question but does not as such know the answer to any "what is" question, for instance to the question "What is a god?"

There follows, as one might expect, the inquiry regarding justice. The question "what is justice?" or "who is a just man?" is not raised but answered. Socrates speaks first of the noble use of human beings without speaking of justice and then abruptly of obedience to the laws or justice: can the noble use of human beings be fully understood in terms of obedience to the laws? The result corresponds to the result regarding piety: just are those who know what is lawful regarding human beings; a man who knows what is lawful regarding human beings necessarily acts justly. (Contrast this with IV.2.20.) Euthydemos, who was present at the conversation with Hippias or an equivalent, knows now what kind of things is called just, namely, those commanded by the laws.

One might expect Xenophon to turn next to continence or moderation (cf. III.9.4). Yet not altogether unexpectedly he does not do this but instead turns to wisdom. Here Socrates directs the inquiry more completely than in the two preceding cases. Wisdom proves to be science (*episteme*) of the beings, of all beings. We recall that Socrates never ceased considering what each of the beings is: considering each of the beings means trying to understand all beings. What Socrates understood by "beings," becomes clear from the examples. He did not consider each act of piety or justice for example but "what piety is" and "what justice is": he considered the whole tribe or kind of pious or of just things, that which holds together all pious or all just things; he thus separated from one another the pious and the just things for instance; but he considered in this manner all beings as distinct from one another and as parts of the whole (cf. I.1.14). "All beings" thus understood are truly "the most excellent things" spoken of toward the end of the preceding chapter. According to Euthydemos, no man is able to understand all beings. Yet at any rate, a man is wise in regard to that which he understands. When discussing piety and justice Socrates had spoken, not of understanding but of knowing (*eidenai*) and believing (*oiesthai*).

At the beginning of the next inquiry Socrates addresses Euthydemos by name, something he had not done in this chapter except at the beginning of the inquiry regarding piety and which he will do only once more in the chapter. We draw from this the tentative conclusion that Xenophon's account of Socrates' training Euthydemos in dialectics consists of three main parts, the first of them including, if not consisting of, the inquiry regarding piety and justice.

The two inquiries following the inquiry on wisdom deal with the good and the beautiful (noble). Since wisdom is concerned with the beings only, it would seem that wisdom is not concerned with the good and beautiful things as such (cf. II.1.27–28). For the good things are not good for everyone and always and the beautiful things are beautiful relative to their purposes, which vary, but the beings are beings simply. For instance, the "what is" of piety, justice, and so on is always the same. The good is primarily what is good for a given individual in these or those circumstances, but being is primarily the "what" of a class or tribe of beings. The good and noble things are the objects, not of *sophia* (wisdom), but of *phronesis* (good sense) (cf. IV.8.11). The Socrates of the bulk of the *Memorabilia* is *phronimos* but not *sophos:* the conceal-ment of Socrates' *sophia* is *the* defense of Socrates.

In the exchange with Aristippos, Socrates had explicitly identified the good and the beautiful while in the subsequent speech he had tacitly distinguished the beautiful as the pleasant from the good as the useful (III.8.5–10; cf. also IV.3.5). Now he identifies the good with the helpful (*ophelimon*) and the beautiful with the useful (*chresimon*), and he is altogether silent on the pleasant. What is good for one man may some-times be bad for another. As we have seen, even the greatest good is not good for all men in all circumstances. Freedom is most noble for man (IV.5.2–5), yet for some men it is good to be enslaved by the right kind of people (*Oeconomicus* I.23). What is good and beautiful, as distinguished from what is just, is not determined by the laws.

Finally, Socrates discusses courage or manliness with Eu-thydemos. In this case too, it appears, just as in the cases of piety and justice, that virtue is knowledge: courage is knowl-edge of the terrible or dangerous things. There is however one crucial difference between courage and those two virtues: courage has no relation to law in the sense that the terrible and dangerous things are not as such disclosed by the laws. We should also note that in attempting to define piety and justice Socrates had not spoken of the impious and unjust, whereas in the present case he speaks of both the courageous and the cowardly: both the courageous and the cowardly be-have toward the terrible and dangerous things as they be-lieve they ought to behave toward them. We understand from this why there can be impious and unjust people: knowing the laws as well as the pious and just do, they believe it to be to their advantage to act impiously and unjustly and hence that they ought to act impiously and unjustly, for all choose what they believe to be most advantageous to themselves (III.9.4).

We must not forget to note that in the present chapter, as distinguished from the parallel in III.9, there is no explicit mention of virtue; i.e., piety, justice, and wisdom are not said to be good. Piety had not been mentioned in the parallel.

It may be presumed that the definitions given in III.9 which are not restated in IV.6—the definitions of madness, envy, leisure, doing well, and being lucky—retain their force.

Xenophon adds two remarks to his account of Socrates' training Euthydemos in dialectics: one about what Socrates believed regarding the various regimes, and another about Socrates' dialectics in general. These remarks no longer reproduce what Socrates said with a view to Euthydemos. In III.9, where Socrates was said to have said that every virtue is wisdom, he was accordingly said to have said that only those are kings and rulers who understand how to rule, while the manner in which they came to power was treated as irrelevant. Now, after we have received an inkling of what wisdom as distinguished from the other virtues is, we learn not what Socrates said but what he believed or held (*enomize*) regarding kingship and rule: he no longer disregards the laws (*nomoi*), as he had done in the earlier treatment. Kingship, he held, is rule over willing subjects and in accordance with the laws of the city, while tyranny is rule over unwilling subjects and not according to laws but as it pleases the tyrant. Where the ruling offices are filled from among those who perfect or complete what is established by law or custom, from among the equitable (*epieikeis*), the regime is an aristocracy, while where they are filled on the basis of property assessments, it is a plutocracy, and where the office holders are chosen from all, it is a democracy. One must wonder whether the distinction between kingship and tyranny does not apply to republican government as well. Xenophon's silence about laws when speaking of plutocracy and democracy suggests an affirmative answer (cf. I.2.40–45 and *Hellenica* II.3.16). Or does the distinction between regal and tyrannical rule apply to all kinds of governments, aristocracy included? Aristocratic government will be tyrannical if its subjects obey it despite its excellence against their wills.

When someone contradicted Socrates regarding any subject without having anything clear to say, he led the discussion up to the assumption (*hypothesis*) on which it was based by questioning the contradictor. In this manner the truth became manifest to the very contradictors. But when he himself went through a subject, i.e., when he taught (cf. Plato, *Meno* 84d1–2), he made his way through the things regarding which there was the broadest agreement; he held that this procedure made the speech safe. Hence he established agreement among the listeners to a much higher degree than anyone else whom Xenophon knew. Socrates said that Homer too attributed to Odysseus the quality of being a safe speaker (*rhetor*) as being able to conduct his speech through what was commonly accepted by human beings (cf. Isocrates, *Antidosis* 143). Socratic dialectic was then twofold: he proceeded differently when he talked to a "contradictor" from how he did when he talked to non-"contradictors"; only the former procedure led to the truth, while the latter led to agreement on the basis of generally accepted opinions or to concord. It is easy to see the connection between this distinction, however vague, and the distinction between the good natures and those natures that are not good. The Odyssean kind of dialectics is characteristic of the good citizen but the good citizen, as is indicated in this very context, is not the same as a wise man doing the work peculiar to the wise man. It makes sense to call the Odyssean dialectics rhetoric. If this is so, Socrates did teach rhetoric and not merely dialectics strictly understood. Perhaps Xenophon was thinking of the Odyssean kind of dialectics when he said that Socrates made his companions skilled in "contriving." At any rate we understand now better why Socrates frequently quoted the verses in which Homer presents Odysseus as talking differently to outstanding men and to common men (I.2.58).

At the beginning of his account of Socrates' twofold dialectics Xenophon indicates that wisdom, the skill of the statesman, and courage are three different things. (Cf. Plato, *Sophist* 217a–b3.)

IV.7. Socrates also took care that his companions be self-sufficient to perform the suitable actions (for while continence is necessary for being good at doing, it is not sufficient), i.e., the actions suitable to gentlemen. What he himself knew of those things he taught most eagerly; but as for matters in which he was rather inexperienced he took his companions to the experts. One might think that what is most suitable for gentlemen to understand is the military art and the art of farming. But this is not what Xenophon has in mind here. He begins the chapter as follows: "That Socrates made known his thought simply with a view to those who consorted with him, seems to me to be manifest from what has been said." This sentence is by no means ironical in the now common meaning of the term: Socrates did make known simply, straightforwardly his thought with a view to the nature of his interlocutors; i.e., he set it forth manifoldly, for "he did not approach all in the same manner" (IV.1.3). What Xenophon seems to suggest in the sentence quoted is that Socrates thought nothing, that he knew nothing but what he set forth without any concealment. Yet, as he makes clear in the immediate sequel, Socrates knew things which he did not teach. This applies in particular to geometry and, above all, to astronomy. He taught that gentlemen should study these disciplines only to the extent to which they are useful, i.e., that they should study only the rudiments; in that study he even joined his companions; i.e., he taught those rudiments. Yet he himself was not unfamiliar with the higher themes treated by these disciplines. But he discouraged his companions from studying them because they are useless and, as far as astronomy is concerned, in addition even impious: one does not please gods by investigating what they did not wish to reveal. Now the god did not wish to reveal how he contrives the particulars of the heavenly things: no one ought to think that he will become good at contriving by finding out how the gods contrive the heavenly things. Yet, we must wonder, must one not investigate the god's or the gods' contrivances in order to convince oneself or others of the existence of gods (cf. I.4.7) or to refute the insane assertions of Anaxagoras regarding the sun or even to understand those assertions?

Socrates disparaged the higher studies as unattainable and useless superhuman wisdom. But a man may fairly wish to possess superhuman wisdom that would help him. Socrates would advise such a man to employ divination, for he who knows through what means the gods give signs to human beings regarding affairs would never, he said, be deprived of the counsel of gods. He did not obtrude his *daimonion* (cf. I.1.4).

IV.8. Someone might go further and say that Socrates' claim regarding his *daimonion* was refuted by his condemnation: ought the *daimonion* not have told him how he could escape that condemnation? Thus Xenophon returns at the end to the theme with which he began. He refutes the alleged refutation by the consideration that Socrates was quite old when he was indicted and would have died anyway not much later; besides, he thus escaped not only the decline of his reasoning power but exhibited the strength of his soul by the manner in which he conducted himself at his trial and while he waited for his execution; he thus died in the manner that is most noble, most happy, and most dear to the gods. If facing death nobly is courage or manliness, Socrates was singularly manly. To establish his defense of Socrates' *daimonion* still more firmly, Xenophon reports what Socrates had said shortly before his trial to Hermogenes, an indigent but pious man (II.10.2–3; *Symposium* 3.14, 4.46–48). Hermogenes told Socrates that he ought to think about what he would say in his defense. Socrates replied first that he had done nothing throughout his life but examine thoroughly the just things and the unjust ones and do the former while abstaining from the latter. It is unlikely that Socrates understands here by the just things the legal things. When Hermogenes reminded him of the fact that the Athenian judges had often been induced by speeches both to condemn the innocent and to acquit the guilty, Socrates told him that the *daimonion* opposed his attempt to think of his defense before the judges; the *daimonion*, or the god, obviously agreed with the view stated by Socrates that it was time for him to die and that he had hitherto lived as well and as pleasantly as any man; for those live best who take care in the best manner to become as good as possible and those live most pleasantly who sense to the highest degree that they are becoming better. This statement regarding the difference between the good and the pleasant is obviously incomplete but it reveals what this difference is on the highest level: the greatest good is wisdom and the greatest pleasure is one's awareness of one's progress in wisdom. We also note that the *daimonion* did not, in this case at any rate, tell Socrates anything that he would not have been able to tell himself. If he lived longer, Socrates continued, it would perhaps be necessary for him to see and hear less well and to weaken in his intellectual power and in his memory, and hence to live both worse and less pleasantly. Socrates adds "perhaps" because he does not know whether he might not live some more years in full possession of the powers mentioned; the *daimonion* did not reveal to him anything on this point, perhaps because it is not knowable in advance. Why should he not then wish to prolong his life? He would wish for it if it could be obtained justly and honorably but there was no prospect of this.

Xenophon concludes the *Memorabilia* appropriately with a eulogy of Socrates. He enumerates therein Socrates' virtues, and in the first place the three virtues discussed in IV.3–5 in the order in which they were discussed there; yet he omits now any reference to law when speaking of piety and justice: Socrates was pious since he did nothing without the counsel of the gods, i.e., without the use of divination (IV.7.10), i.e., of his *daimonion*. On the other hand however he replaces wisdom as the science of all beings by prudence (*phronesis*) as the ability to distinguish infallibly between the better and the worse things. Although Socrates was said shortly before to have died the most noble death, courage or manliness is not mentioned among his virtues, either because he was not the kind of man to take unusual risks for the sake of freedom from tyranny (cf. I.2.32–38 with *Hiero* 5.1) or because he lacked the virtue of the man (*aner*) which includes surpassing one's enemies in harming them.

Apology of Socrates to the Jury

Xenophon's title *Apology of Socrates to the Jury* implies that there was another defense of Socrates. This implication is made explicit near the beginning of the work: Socrates has spent his whole life in caring for his defense by never doing anything unjust. His whole life was his defense in deed, while his defense to the jury was his defense in speech.

The purpose of the work is to show that Socrates' *megalegoria* ("talking big") in his defense to the jury was sensible by setting forth the deliberation about his defense and the end of his life—a deliberation that issued in his *megalegoria*. That deliberation is also set forth—although not as deliberation—in the last chapter of the *Memorabilia* but there it is presented in order to show that Socrates' condemnation does not refute his claim regarding his *daimonion* or in order to justify his *daimonion;* here it is presented in order to justify his *megalegoria*.

Let us first consider Socrates' *megalegoria*. In order to appreciate it properly, one must compare his refutation of the indictment with the refutation given by Xenophon in his own name in the first two chapters of the *Memorabilia*. In this comparison I shall speak as if I knew that Xenophon had written the *Memorabilia* before he wrote the *Apology of Socrates*. I do not possess such knowledge but I express myself in the manner indicated because it is convenient.

Xenophon quotes in the *Apology of Socrates* the text of the indictment on the whole as he had quoted it in the *Memorabilia* but he does not make it as clear now as he had made it then that the indictment consisted of two parts (the impiety charge and the corruption charge); in accordance with this, his Socrates already speaks of his character in refuting the impiety charge while Xenophon had done so only when refuting the corruption charge.

His Socrates' reply to the impiety charge agrees with Xenophon's refutation of it to the extent that it speaks of Socrates' sacrificing and of his *daimonion*. But while Xenophon speaks of Socrates' sacrificing both at home and on the common altars of the city, Socrates speaks only of his sacrificing at the common festivals and on the public altars; he is silent on his strictly private sacrifices at home; he makes the jury wonder whether he performed this particular kind of act of piety only when he could be seen by everybody. He is also silent on the fact treated by Xenophon at some length, that he did not study the nature of all things but considered always the human things. As for the *daimonion*, he describes it as a voice of a god, as a sound, he compares it to other kinds of divination by sounds, and he shows that divination by sounds is used by other people as well; in the center of his argument he raises the rhetorical question as to whether anyone will dispute to thunders that they are sounds or that they are a very great omen. He concludes his statement on his *daimonion* just as Xenophon did, by saying that the divine advice which he communicated to his "friends" was never found to be erroneous (except that Xenophon speaks of "companions"). At this point he was interrupted by the clamor of the jury and perhaps for this reason prevented from mentioning the fact, mentioned by Xenophon, that he sometimes sent his acquaintances to public oracles.

The jury were annoyed by the claim which Socrates had raised on behalf of his *daimonion:* some did not believe him;

others were envious of him because he received from the gods too—not only from nature or from human beings—greater things than they did. The envious ones believed in Socrates' *daimonion:* must they not also have believed in his innocence? By no means, for by believing in Socrates' *daimonion* they did not yet believe that he believed in the gods of the city, and Socrates was accused not of atheism, but of not believing in the gods of the city. At any rate Socrates now addresses those who do not wish to believe that he is honored by gods (*daimones*); he raises still higher claims; he provokes the jury still more; he talks still bigger. Chairephon, he says, once asked in Delphi about him in the presence of many, and Apollon responded that no human being is more liberal, more just, and more moderate than he. Thereupon the jury clamored, as could be expected, still more than before. Socrates appeased them by telling them that the god did not, after all, compare him to a god, as he had done or almost done in the case of Lykourgos, the Spartan legislator. Nevertheless, he goes on, they should not believe the god rashly even in the comparatively small praise he had bestowed on him but should examine it point by point. In the examination Socrates speaks of his continence (without using the word), his liberality, his justice, and his wisdom. The god had been silent on Socrates' wisdom, just as Xenophon had been in the *Memorabilia*. But he had also been silent on Socrates' piety; he could have meant that his piety was part of his moderation (cf. *Memorabilia* IV.3.1–2): but in his examination of the oracle Socrates is silent about his moderation: moderation is the opposite of *hybris* (*Apol. Socr.* 19) and out of place in the context of his *megalegoria*. By justice he means here, not law-abidingness (*Memorabilia* IV.4) nor helping others (*Memorabilia* IV.8.11) but not needing anything belonging to others. We understand now why he did not speak of sending his acquaintances to public oracles: he did not send Chairephon to Delphi to ask the god about him. We also understand why Socrates speaks of his virtues or his way of life while refuting the impiety charge.

Socrates next gives proofs that he had not toiled in vain in his quest for wisdom as well as in the practice of the other virtues mentioned, without mentioning any of the particular virtues by name. Accordingly he speaks now of his helpfulness to others. He points out the contrast between his self-sufficiency and the others' lack of it; in particular he refused to accept gifts although many desired to give him things; one is tempted to say that he lived like a god among human beings. It must have been particularly galling to his listeners to hear that during the siege (when Athens was starved into surrender) "the others" pitied themselves while he was in no way in greater straits than when the city was at the height of her prosperity. He draws the conclusion that he is justly praised by both gods and men.

He then turns to the corruption charge. He points out that this part of Meletos' charge is strikingly at variance with his practice of the virtues mentioned or indicated. The charge presupposes that we know what the corruptions of the young are. Socrates does not cross-examine Meletos on this question. He assumes that corrupting means causing someone pious to become unholy, someone moderate to become a man of insolent pride, someone living temperately to become extravagant, a moderate drinker to become a drunkard, a lover of toil to become soft, and the like. Meletos is unable to name a single youth whom Socrates has corrupted in this sense. Instead he claims to know some whom Socrates has persuaded to obey him rather than their parents. Socrates grants that he has done so as regards education but asserts that in doing so he merely has followed the maxim that one should obey experts rather than parents: men obey physicians, political leaders, and generals rather than their parents; they prefer those experts to their parents. "All Athenians obey in the Assemblies those who speak most sensibly rather than their relatives." This statement is obviously too sanguine; Socrates corrects it therefore when speaking of the generals: the Athenians elect as generals those whom they believe to be most sensible in matters of war. His own case differs from that of the other experts in two points. First, he is an expert in education, which is the greatest good for human beings, greater than health, the well-being of the city, and victory; it is not the greatest good simply, which is wisdom (*Memorabilia* IV.5.6): the gods are wise but not in need of education. Second, he is preferred as an expert in education not by "the Athenians" but by "some" who are partly Athenians and partly foreigners (17; cf. *Memorabilia* III.11.17). When Xenophon refuted the corruption charge, he defended Socrates against the accusation that he subverted the authority of the fathers; Socrates defends himself against the accusation that he subverted the authority of the parents, i.e., fathers and mothers. We must leave it open whether this change is also caused by his *megalegoria;* in order to reach a decision, one would have to consider the Socratic conversation dealing with the proper conduct toward one's mother (*Memorabilia* II.2). Let no one say that Socrates replied to Meletos, who had spoken of the parents, while Xenophon replies to the unnamed accuser who had spoken of the fathers, for it was the same Xenophon who chose the different wordings for the different occasions.

This is the whole defense of Socrates to the jury. His refutation of the impiety charge is more than twice as long as his refutation of the corruption charge; the opposite proportion obtains between the two parts of Xenophon's refutation: Socrates treats the more credible charge much more extensively than the less credible one (cf. *Memorabilia* I.1.20–2.1). This too is a sign of his *megalegoria*.

After his condemnation he addressed the jury again. He first contrasts the impiety and injustice of those who brought about his condemnation with his innocence: he had not been shown to sacrifice to new *daimones* instead of Zeus, Hera, and the gods associated with them, nor to swear by, nor to name other gods; and how could he corrupt the young since he accustomed them to endurance and frugality? nor was he even accused of having committed any action which is capitally punished. Xenophon draws the same distinction between the things of which Socrates was accused and the actions which are capitally punished (*Memorabilia* I.2.62–63). But Xenophon draws a further distinction between those actions and inflicting evils on the city like being responsible for the loss of a war or for sedition or for treason. Socrates does not make the latter distinction but adds treason to the actions which are capitally punished; both he and Xenophon are silent on sedition as a capital crime of which Socrates was not even accused; Socrates' silence is more suggestive than Xenophon's since Socrates mentions treason, but not sedition, as a capital crime of which he was not even accused. (For the interpretation consider *Memorabilia* I.2.9–11.) Socrates continues by expressing his astonishment about how in the world his action deserving death has been shown to the jury. His unjustly dying is disgraceful not to him but to those who condemned him. He refers to the posthumous fame of Palamedes, who is up to the present day the theme of much more noble hymns than Odysseus, for Odysseus killed him unjustly; he predicts that the same illustrious fate will fall to him. He does not state here why Odysseus destroyed Palamedes. In the *Memorabilia* (IV.2.33) he says that Odysseus destroyed Palamedes because he envied him for his wisdom: Socrates was condemned to death because those who condemned him envied him for his wisdom (cf. *Education of Cyrus* III.1.38–39; *Kynegetikos* 1.11). He does not spell this out because comparing Meletos and his ilk to Odysseus would be altogether absurd, although the other possible implication, namely, that Odysseus, even Odysseus, would have envied Socrates for his wisdom, would be most suitable to his *megalegoria*. The true reason appears from Xenophon's remark near the end of the *Apology of Socrates* (32) that Socrates made himself envied because he extolled himself before the court and thus increased the willingness of the jury to condemn him: the jury envied him less for his wisdom than for his provocative high-mindedness. In other words, his claim to be wise would not be an act of *megalegoria*. At the end of his remarks to the jury he speaks of the benefactions which he had bestowed on those who had conversations with him: he does not speak here of his having helped others by his deeds (cf. *Memorabilia* I.3.1 and IV.8.11).

Xenophon claims to have heard from Hermogenes what Socrates said to the jury. But what Socrates said to the jury is only a part of what Hermogenes told Xenophon and of the *Apology of Socrates* as a whole. We must now consider the other part, which partly agrees with the last chapter of the *Memorabilia*. We must be open to the possibility that the differences between that part of the *Apology of Socrates* and the last chapter of the *Memorabilia* stem from the presence of Socrates' *megalegoria* in the former and its absence from the latter.

In the last chapter of the *Memorabilia* Xenophon shows first in his own name that Socrates' dying at the time of his

life at which he died was best for him and, above all, that the
manner in which he bore death was of the utmost nobility.
He mentions there among other things that he pleaded his
cause "most truthfully, most liberally, and most justly"; the
claim of the truthfulness of Socrates' plea is not raised in the
Apology of Socrates and in particular not by Socrates himself.
Xenophon turns next to what he had heard about him from
Hermogenes, the son of Hipponikos. Hermogenes was a particularly pious man (*Symposium* 4.46–49). In the *Apology of
Socrates* Xenophon turns to Hermogenes' report immediately
after he has stated the purpose of the work; he does not say
now that he has "heard" it from Hermogenes; in the *Memorabilia* he eventually says that the conversation which Hermogenes reported took place between Socrates and "Hermogenes
and the others." He vouches then less for the authenticity of
the version given in the *Apology of Socrates* than for the authenticity of the version given in the last chapter of the
Memorabilia. When Hermogenes asked Socrates whether he
ought not to think of his defense, he replied that his whole life
was his defense, for, as the *Apology of Socrates* has it, he had
not done anything unjust, or, as the *Memorabilia* has it, he
had not done anything but consider the just and the unjust
things and done the just things while abstaining from the unjust ones: in the *Apology* version of the conversation with
Hermogenes he is silent about what he did do. Hermogenes
tried to persuade him to think of his defense by reminding him
of how easily the Athenian juries can be swayed by speech
to condemn the innocent and to acquit the guilty; the *Apology*
speaks in somewhat greater detail than the *Memorabilia* of the
effect which speech can have in bringing about the acquittal
of the guilty. Socrates replied that when he tried to think of
his defense, the *daimonion* opposed it; according to the *Apol-*

ogy the *daimonion* opposed it twice. Hermogenes found this action of the *daimonion* strange; to this the Socrates of the *Memorabilia* replied with the question whether he finds it strange that the god thinks that it is time for Socrates to die; the Socrates of the *Apology* replied with the question whether he finds it strange that the god too thinks that it is time for Socrates to die; according to the *Apology* the god merely confirmed the result of what Socrates himself had thought before, of his own deliberation: the theme of the *Apology*, but not of the *Memorabilia*, is Socrates' deliberation about his defense and the end of his life. The deliberation consists of a comparison between the life he has led hitherto and the life he can still expect. In both versions he speaks of the goodness and of the pleasantness of his previous life but the two versions differ regarding the source or the content of his pleasure. According to the *Memorabilia* his pleasure consisted in his awareness of his becoming better; according to the *Apology* he derived his greatest pleasure from his knowledge that he had lived his whole life in a holy and just manner and as a consequence he admired himself strongly. One does not do full justice to this difference by saying that according to the *Memorabilia* his life was a progress, while according to the *Apology* it was not a progress. In the *Memorabilia* he contrasts, and in the *Apology* he does not contrast, his friends with other men's friends. If he were to live longer, he knows that his sight, his hearing, his ability to learn, and his memory of what he had learned, would necessarily decline (*Apology*) or that his sight, his hearing, his reasoning, his ability to learn, and his memory would perhaps necessarily decline (*Memorabilia*): the *Apology* is silent about the expected decline of his reasoning. This particular *megalegoria* has been prepared by those peculiarities of the *Apology* which apparently stem from the opposite of

megalegoria, namely, his silence on the core of his life. (Xenophon himself speaks only of the decline of reasoning, i.e., of
the decline most sensible to Socrates' companions.) Accordingly, the *Memorabilia* speaks, and the *Apology* does not speak,
of how bad it is to be unaware of one's decline. The *Apology*
says, and the *Memorabilia* does not say, that Socrates' death,
apart from its coming in time, also comes in the easiest manner
(he means by drinking the hemlock): in this point too the
god's voice, or the gods, confirmed Socrates' deliberation;
Xenophon speaking in his own name also says in the *Apology*
that Socrates suffered the easiest of deaths. Tht *Apology* speaks
only of the easy character of Socrates' death; the *Memorabilia*
speaks only of its noble character. In the *Apology* Socrates
speaks so powerfully of the misery of old age and illness that
he feels compelled to add that he will accept his condemnation
as the unintended effect of his stating his opinion about himself
and that he refuses to beg meanly for his life: he will not
deliberately bring about his condemnation. In the *Memorabilia*
however he is said to have said—and this concludes Xenophon's
report there about what Socrates said to Hermogenes and the
others—that his unjust condemnation is disgraceful only to
his condemners and that his posthumous fame will vindicate
him; according to the *Apology* Socrates said these things at
the end of his second speech to the jury. In the *Apology* Xenophon's report of Hermogenes' report continues so as to include
the report about what Socrates said to the jury both before
and after the condemnation.

Xenophon inserts between Socrates' two speeches to the jury
a remark which he does not ascribe to any source. Socrates and
his friends have said at the trial more than he has reported.
With a view to what did he make his selection? From the beginning of the *Apology* one would expect that he selected

what would show most clearly Socrates' *megalegoria* and its reasonable ground, namely, his holding the view that at his age death is preferable for him to life. Now he says that he made his selection in order to show that Socrates was concerned above all with appearing neither impious nor unjust; and he did not believe that he should hold out against dying: Xenophon replaces *megalegoria* by the overriding concern with not appearing to be impious or unjust; *megalegoria* and what replaces it are interchangeable. These two things, Xenophon continues, became still clearer after his condemnation. In the first place, he refused to propose a counterpenalty on the ground that to make such a proposal would be tantamount to admitting guilt. Secondly, when his comrades wished to steal him away from prison, he did not follow them but even seemed to make fun of them by asking them whether they knew a place outside of Attika to which death has no access. One must wonder whether the first of these two facts must not be explained by his *megalegoria* or the purpose which it served. At any rate in the peroration Xenophon praises Socrates, not for his piety and justice, but for his wisdom and nobility; by "nobility" we may have to understand here his outstanding usefulness combined with his gentleness (cf. *Oeconomicus* XV.4).

After having completed his, or Hermogenes', report of what Socrates said to the jury, Xenophon reports three more utterances of Socrates without indicating a determinate source; perhaps these utterances were not reported to him by Hermogenes. (1) When those who accompanied him after the trial wept, he asked them why they wept just now; did they not know for a long time that since he was born he was condemned by nature to die? (2) When his silly lover Apollodoros said he found it hardest to bear that he saw him die unjustly,

Socrates said, stroking Apollodoros' head: Would you prefer that I die justly? and at the same time he laughed. This is the only occasion when the Xenophontic Socrates is explicitly said to have smiled or laughed. (3) When he saw Anytos, proud of his victory over Socrates, pass by, he told how he had blamed him for the bad education he was giving to his son. Availing himself of a privilege which according to Homer some men who are about to die enjoy, he prophesied that owing to his bad education Anytos' son, despite some gifts, would fall victim to some disgraceful desire. Xenophon adds that this prophecy came true. One might say that Socrates' utterance about Anytos was his revenge on him and therefore that on this occasion and only on this occasion Socrates revealed himself to possess the virtue of a man (*aner*) which consists in surpassing not merely one's friends in doing them good but also one's enemies in doing them harm (*Memorabilia* II.6.35). He surely acts the part of the expert in education who questions the authority of the parents in this respect. None of the three utterances establishes Socrates' piety.

≈≈≈≈≈ *Symposium*

Chapter 1

The *Symposium* is not as simply a Socratic writing as the *Memorabilia*, the *Oeconomicus*, and the *Apology of Socrates*. As Xenophon says in the opening sentence, the work presents a particularly memorable example of playful deeds of perfect gentlemen; Socrates is only one of these gentlemen. The *Symposium* belongs as much, almost as much, with the *Hellenica* as with the three other Socratic writings, for the *Hellenica* deals with the serious deeds of gentlemen, as Xenophon shows silently by regarding his accounts of those notorious non-gentlemen, the tyrants, as excursuses (VI.1.9 and 5.1; VII.3.4 and 4.1). The *Hellenica* transmits a playful utterance of Theramenes (II.3, end); but the circumstances in which that utterance was made were of deadly seriousness. Four of the characters of the *Symposium* (Kallias, Socrates, Charmides, and Nikeratos) occur also in the *Hellenica*. The serious deeds of the perfect gentleman Ischomachos which are rehearsed in the *Oeconomicus* (XI.1), being economic rather than political, lack the obvious gravity of the deeds recorded in the *Hellenica*.

This is not meant to deny the obvious fact that the *Symposium* is a Socratic writing. The fact that at the beginning Socrates comes to sight as only one of many gentlemen engaging in playful deeds, only slightly conceals the fact that the work presents above all the playful deeds of Socrates: Socrates proves to be the central character. The work must therefore be seen in the context of the Socratic writings and more par-

143

ticularly of the Socratic writings other than the *Memorabilia*. Seen in that context the *Symposium* reveals itself as devoted not merely to Socrates' playful deeds but simply to his deeds: his deed, as distinguished from his speech and his thought, is nothing but playful (cf. *Memorabilia* III.11.16).

Xenophon claims to have been present at the banquet.

The banquet was not altogether planned. Kallias happened to be in love with the boy Autolykos. Autolykos had been victorious in the pankration. (He won his victory one or two years after Aristophanes had exhibited the *Clouds*.) Kallias had taken him to look at the horse race. After the horse race he went with him and his father to his house in the Peiraieus; Nikeratos also went along with him. Then Kallias happened to see Socrates, Kritoboulos, Hermogenes, Antisthenes, and Charmides; we do not know whether Socrates and his companions had been looking at the race. When Kallias saw Socrates and his group, he ordered someone to conduct Autolykos and his group to his house and approached Socrates and his group telling them that he was about to entertain Autolykos and his father. It would not be fair to say that he treated Nikeratos as negligible. Surely Xenophon himself treats himself as still more negligible. We remember how badly he treated himself in the *Memorabilia* (I.3.8–13). Yet precisely the way in which he treated himself in the *Memorabilia* could encourage one to say that he presented himself in the *Symposium* as an invisible and inaudible participant who did not partake of food and drink and who was not invited.

In inviting Socrates and his group, Kallias says that his halls would be more splendidly adorned by men with purified souls like them than by generals and other actual or would-be dignitaries. Socrates pretends to notice in this apparent compliment a sign of Kallias' constant contempt for him and his like:

Kallias, the pupil of Protagoras, Gorgias, Prodikos, and many others looks down on "us," who cannot buy wisdom but have to strive for it in the sweat of their brows. For Kallias, Socrates is just one gentleman among many: he addresses all five men equally. He tries to entice them to accept his invitation by promising to exhibit to them the many wise things which he possesses. They first politely decline but then accept when Kallias seems to be hurt.

After they all had taken their seats, the first thing that struck and affected all of them was Autolykos' beauty, which was conjoined with bashfulness and moderation. On reflection one could think that such beauty is by nature regal. Hardly less worth seeing was Kallias, possessed as he was by the god Eros as the god of sober (*sōphrōn*) love.

The dinner would have been eaten in perfect, almost awed silence but for the sudden unplanned appearance of Philippos the jester, who came uninvited. (One cannot exclude the possibility that his apparently unplanned appearance was arranged beforehand between him and Kallias.) His appearance gave Kallias an occasion for a mild pleasantry which, he hoped, would impress Autolykos. Philippos made two jests without inciting anyone to laugh; only when he wept about his failure in his profession did Kritoboulos, that lover of comedy (*Oeconomicus* III.7), burst out into loud laughter.

"Beauty and love," "laughter," and "wisdom" are the three themes of the work.

Chapter 2

After the dinner there appeared a Syracusan fellow bringing with him a girl good at flute playing, a dancing girl skilled in exhibiting spectacular performances, and a very pretty boy who was excellent in cither playing and dancing. Their appearance was obviously planned. It is not altogether surprising that for the time being only the flutist and the boy performed. After their performance Socrates, availing himself of his natural ascendancy, praised Kallias for the enjoyment he had provided for their palates, their eyes, and their ears. Kallias as a good host was not too eager to exhibit the many wise things he possessed. He proposed therefore that they should in addition be supplied with the enjoyment of perfume but Socrates firmly refused: men, free men, ought to smell of gymnastic exertions and their accompaniments. Lykon, Autolykos' father, wondered of what older men should smell. "Of perfect gentlemanship, by Zeus," Socrates rejoined, of an odor, as he explained to Lykon with the help of a quotation from Theognis, that is acquired through associating with the right kind of man through learning from them. Lykon drew his son's attention to what Socrates had said or quoted. Socrates assured him that his son is already acting upon it, as he shows in particular by associating with his father. His half-attempt to support the authority of the fathers—the primary teachers of virtue—was followed by a dissension regarding the availability of teachers of virtue and the teachability of virtue. At Socrates' suggestion they dropped the subject for the time being because it is controversial, and completed the task at hand, for the dancing girl —the central performer—was about to begin an act to the accompaniment of the flutist. The act—quite an achievement— led Socrates to observe that the female nature is in no respect inferior to the male except in judgment and strength; therefore everyone who has a wife should confidently teach her what he would like her to know in order to use her. Has the teachability of virtue ceased to be controversial? Or have the things which dancing girls learn from dancing masters and wives from their husbands nothing to do with virtue? Socrates' exhortation induced Antisthenes to ask him why he had not educated Xanthippe but lives with her who is of all wives present, past, and future the most difficult, as she is. Socrates replied that he does this for the same reason for which men who wish to become expert horsemen choose high-spirited horses: he who succeeds in the most difficult case will succeed in all other cases; Socrates, wishing to live with human beings, chose Xanthippe because if he will bridle or bear her, he will easily manage all other human beings. Antisthenes' question shows that Socrates was not conspicuously successful in managing Xanthippe; the teachability of virtue is still controversial. As Xenophon puts it, Socrates' reply seemed to have been right on target. Next the dancing girl performed entirely by herself an act so dangerous that the spectators trembled for her. Thereupon Socrates addressed to Antisthenes this remark: at least the viewers of that spectacle will no longer deny, he believes, that even manliness is teachable, even to a woman. The controversial issue is settled: virtue is teachable. Antisthenes drew the necessary conclusion: the Syracusan is a teacher at any rate of manliness; by exhibiting to the city the dancing girl's act, he could well tell the Athenians that for payment he would make all Athenians—including their womenfolk?—face their enemy in battle. Philippos however was amused by the thought that even a demagogue of notorious cowardice might learn the dangerous act of the dancing girl: no one laughed about this joke conceived in the spirit of popular comedy. Then the boy danced. Socrates admired how the boy's beauty was farther enhanced by his dancing. Charmides divined that this was a praise of the dancing master. Socrates was indeed willing to learn from him the postures exhibited by the boy, and he had that wish because he wished to dance. When he said this, all laughed. (The contrast between the effect of Socrates' statement and that of Philippos' jest could not have been greater: Socrates is much better at making people of some refinement laugh than any professional jester. Socrates has easily won the silent contest in jesting with Philippos.) But the fact that all laughed does not prove that all laughed for the right reason: Socrates had not expressed a desire to be taught the dangerous act of the dancing girl, i.e., manliness. He wished to learn to dance in order, not to enhance his beauty —for he was not beautiful in the first place—but to increase his suppleness. With a very serious face he explained that he wishes to learn to dance for a variety of reasons, one of them being that for dancing, as distinguished from gymnastic exercises, he would not need a partner nor would he have to strip in public but could do it in the privacy of his home. Those reasons were so powerful that he was already dancing (doubtless in an amateurish way) before he had ever seen the Syracusan and his work; Charmides had caught him dancing in the early morning just the other day; he first feared that Socrates was mad but when he heard his reasons for doing it he went home in order, not indeed to dance, but to do the closest approximation to it of which he was capable; like Socrates, it seems, he did not need a partner. Then Philippos made another jest which remained as ineffective as the preceding one. But Kallias asked Socrates to permit him to learn dancing together with him so that he would stand vis-à-vis Socrates as a partner: he had failed to understand the strictly private, partnerless character of Socrates' dancing.

The performance of the dancing girl and the boy had led to very different reactions on the part of Socrates; the second reaction had caused general laughter. So Philippos imitated the two dancers in a most laughable manner. This time he was entirely successful; as Kallias said, they had become thirsty because they had laughed so much about him. He did not say that they all laughed: did Socrates laugh? Philippos' performance—in contradistinction to the performances which he parodied—did not induce anyone to draw a serious-playful lesson from it. But Socrates approved heartily of the decision to turn to drinking by eloquently praising the gladdening effect of wine, which he compared with the effect of moderate rain on plants; he proposed that they drink not much but often. Philippos improved on his proposal in his manner.

Chapter 3

After they had begun to drink, the flutist played her instrument and the boy played the cither and sang; all applauded. Charmides did more; he praised the gladdening and aphrodisiac effect of the mixture of the young couple's bloom and the music. Socrates was silent on the subject (cf. 8.12) but turned to a higher theme: men like them ought to be able to benefit or to delight one another. Perhaps not all approved of this proposed change but many asked Socrates to explain by what kind of speeches they could benefit or delight one another. He then reminded them of Kallias' promise that he would exhibit to them his wisdom. Kallias was prepared to do this provided everyone else too would bring forward whatever good thing he understood (wisdom is understanding good things). Socrates accepted the condition after having made slight changes: everyone should say what he believes to be the most valuable thing which he understands. Kallias was most proud of his ability to make human beings better, i.e., as Antisthenes found out by questioning him, of his ability to teach them justice; in Antisthenes' view justice is the least disputable kind of gentlemanship, for manliness and wisdom are thought to be sometimes harmful to both friends and the city (hence unjust) whereas justice is never in any respect associated with injustice; he implied that wisdom is at least thought to be compatible with injustice; he was silent on the harm that manliness and wisdom (and justice) can do to their possessor (*Memorabilia* IV.2.33), for the question concerned now the harm to others; he was silent on continence because it was thought to be compatible with greed (*Memorabilia* I.5.3). Kallias then declared that if everyone would say what useful thing he possesses, he would tell him by which art he makes human beings just. The references to understanding and art make one expect that everyone will speak of his particular kind of knowledge as his most valuable possession. This expectation is confirmed by Kallias' asking Nikeratos of which kind of knowledge he is proud. Kallias and Nikeratos are the only two participants who are sons of very wealthy fathers and who had spent a great deal of money to acquire the wisdom or knowledge which they possessed (1.5 and 3.6). Nikeratos was proud of knowing by heart the whole *Iliad* and *Odyssey*. Antisthenes thought that this is nothing to be proud of: all rhapsodes possess that knowledge and they are a tribe of men than which none is sillier. Socrates agreed with Antisthenes: the rhapsodes do not know the hidden meanings; yet, he added, Nikeratos, who had taken lessons from many outstanding men for pay, knows everything that is valuable in Homer. Then he asked Kritoboulos of what he is most proud: he did not ask him of which knowledge or art he is most proud; Kritoboulos was not likely to be most proud of any knowledge or art worth mentioning. Kritoboulos is most proud of his beauty but he thinks, as Socrates learned from him, that he can make, not indeed human beings as such but Socrates and the others better through it. Next he asked Antisthenes of what he is proud. Antisthenes is proud of his wealth. The indigent Hermogenes learns from him that he is extremely poor. Antisthenes will have to explain his paradox. Next Socrates addressed the same question to Charmides. Charmides is proud of his poverty. This statement is not paradoxical since Charmides is in fact poor but is paradoxical for another reason. Therefore Socrates praises poverty, which has this advantage among others, that is it never stolen even if it is left on the street. Kritoboulos, Antisthenes, and Charmides had not boasted of any knowledge or art they possessed. Kallias, who perhaps desired to return to the subject of wisdom, asked Socrates of what he is proud. (This leads to the consequence that Charmides and Socrates, the two men who enjoy partnerless activities, become partners in occupying the central place in this chapter.) With a very solemn face he replied: "Of procuring." Thereupon the company laughed: Socrates' boast is the only one that made them laugh. He does not find his boast laughable, for he could earn much money if he were willing to make use of his art; he is proud of an art. His laughable reply induced Lykon to say that Philippos is obviously proud of his ability to make people laugh; he is, and with greater justice (cf. *Anabasis* V, end) than a certain actor who gives himself airs for his being able to make many people cry. Philippos' boast is in no way paradoxical; it is not even surprising to the meanest capacity; it is obvious even to Lykon. Lykon's intervention has the consequence that the last of the four men who had come with Socrates, namely, Hermogenes, is for the time being forgotten. For Antisthenes now asked Lykon of what he is proud. As they all know, he is proud of his son. This induced someone to say that Autolykos is of course proud of his having been victorious. But Autolykos blushingly and surprisingly denied this; he is proud of his father. This proved to Kallias that Lykon is the wealthiest of men, wealthier even than the Great King. Finally, Nikeratos asked Hermogenes in what he exalts (*agallei*—not, as in all other cases, *mega* or *megiston phroneis*) most; Hermogenes gives the surprising and cryptic answer: in the virtue and power of his friends and in the fact that, being what they are, they take care of him.

While there occur boasts on beauty and laughter, there occur none on wisdom, virtue (gentlemanship), and noble birth, for the company consists of gentlemen.

Chapter 4

After everyone had stated what he is proud of, Socrates said that something is still needed: everyone must prove that what he is proud of deserves being proud of. Kallias is naturally the first to speak. While "you" are perplexed as to "what the just is," he increases the justice of human beings: he is not perplexed as to what justice is. Whom apart from Socrates does he mean when he says that "you" are perplexed as to what justice is? Surely not Antisthenes (cf. 3.4), to say nothing of Lykon and Autolykos. Socrates is amazed by Kallias' claim. Kallias explains that he increases the justice of human beings by giving them money. Antisthenes, taking a very elenctic posture, cross-examines him; he does not ask him, "What is justice?" for he himself is not perplexed in this respect but how he can believe to increase people's justice by giving them money. According to Kallias, many people do mischief (hence are unjust) because of their lack of money: injustice, crime, comes from poverty. Antisthenes forces Kallias to admit that the people to whom he had given money are not grateful to him and some of them even hate him for his benefactions: Kallias can make people just to others but not to himself. Kallias is not impressed by this reasoning but refutes his would-be refuter, whom he apostrophizes as "sophist": just as the wealthy

Kallias can make people just to others but not to himself, indigent house-builders can build houses for others but not for
themselves and live in rented houses. We see that Kallias has
not in vain given much money to men like Protagoras, Gorgias,
and Prodikos (1.5). One must wonder whether Socrates too
did not benefit the city for example and thus increase its justice
without being able to induce the city to treat him justly (*Memorabilia* I.2.61–62). At any rate, he takes the side of Kallias
against Antisthenes by reminding them of the fact that diviners
too are said to be able to predict the future of others but not
to foresee their own. He thus puts an end to this discussion.
Kallias seems to have proven that there is an art by which one
can teach virtue (Cf. 3.4–5 and *On Revenue* 1.1.)

The next speaker is of course Nikeratos. Thanks to his
thorough knowledge of Homer he can make those present
better, for the most wise Homer has dealt in his poems with
almost all human things; whoever of "you" wishes to become
a householder, a public speaker, or a general or similar to
Achilleus, Ajax, Nestor, or Odysseus has only to pay court to
him. Antisthenes asks him whether he also understands how to
rule as a king, i.e., whether he possesses the kingly art which
Socrates was thought to regard as happiness and which he
praised to Euthydemos as the greatest art in order to please
him (*Memorabilia* II.1.17; IV.2.9 and IV.2.11), for Nikeratos
had forgotten to mention Agamemnon, so highly praised by
Homer (*Memorabilia* III.1–2). Antisthenes speaks like the Socrates of the *Memorabilia*. Nikeratos replies very perfunctorily
in the affirmative but turns immediately to other things which
he has learned from the *Iliad*, from which he quotes the praise
of excellent charioteering and the praise of onions as a relish
to drink—a praise most suitable in his opinion to the occasion
of their banquet. No one approves of this praise as Nikeratos

approved and applied it. Charmides suggests that Nikeratos proposes nibbling onions for an un-Homeric reason: he wishes to smell of onions when coming home in order to convince his wife that nobody has even thought of kissing him. Socrates, who enters into the discussion of Homer only at this point, disapproves of their nibbling onions after dinner; they might thus get the reputation of overindulgence. To this it was replied that they should refrain from nibbling onions for a non-Socratic reason; nibbling onions is good for men about to do battle but not for those like them who intend perhaps to kiss someone afterward: Nikeratos himself might desire to kiss his young wife (2.3); his suggestion supported by Homer would be quite unsuitable for him. He has less succeeded in establishing the authority of Homer as the universal teacher than Kallias in establishing his own authority as a teacher of justice.

The next speaker is of course Kritoboulos. His speech and the discussion occasioned by it are by far more extensive than any other speech and the discussion occasioned by it. He explains first on what grounds he is proud of his beauty. The first ground is the gentlemanship of the companions; they always swear that he is beautiful and therefore he believes it. The second ground is that he assumes that, being beautiful, he affects them in the same way in which someone whom he believes to be beautiful affects him. Therefore he regards his beauty as a greater good than the empire of the Great King. He enjoys beholding the beautiful Kleinias more than any other beautiful things that are to be found among humans. (Does he mean to say that the present company enjoy beholding him more than anybody else, for instance, that Kallias enjoys beholding him more than beholding the beautiful Autolykos, with whom he is in love?) Those who are beautiful can acquire the good things by merely being beheld, without

doing anything, while the strong must toil, the manly must in-
cur dangers, and the wise must speak: he would gladly give
his wealth to Kleinias, prefer to be his slave rather than to be
a freeman, and undergo for him any toil and any danger. Since
what is true of the effect of Kleinias on him is true of Kritoboulos' effect on those who love him, he is able to lead human
beings to every virtue—not only to justice—namely, to liberality, love of toil, courage, and indeed sense of shame and
continence; he does not go so far as to claim that he can lead
human beings to wisdom. It is insane, he contends, not to elect
the good-looking as generals; their beauty would achieve what
no art can achieve. The beautiful boy and the beautiful dancing
girl could less be induced by all wise speeches of Socrates to
kiss him than by the silence of the beautiful Kritoboulos to
kiss the latter. Socrates does not call in doubt Kritoboulos'
praise of beauty; he merely questions Kritoboulos' boast that
he is more beautiful than Socrates. According to Kritoboulos,
he would be the ugliest of all the Silenuses in the satyr plays
if he were less beautiful than Socrates. (Was Kritoboulos as
beautiful as he claimed to be? If he was not—cf. Plato, *Eu-
thydemus* 271b2–5—and yet judged correctly his superiority
in beauty to Socrates, Socrates was still uglier than Kritoboulos
says he is.) The matter is of such importance that Xenophon
steps out of his role as a mere reporter of speeches and deeds
and says that Socrates happened indeed to resemble the satyrs.
Socrates does not admit Kritoboulos' superiority; he challenges
him to a beauty contest in which the incorruptible gentlemen
participating in the banquet will be the judges. Kritoboulos
would prefer Kleinias as judge whereupon Socrates rebukes
him for constantly thinking of Kleinias. Kritoboulos defends
himself well enough. Thereupon the grave Hermogenes rebukes Socrates for tolerating Kritoboulos' erotic infatuation.

Socrates defends himself by saying that Kritoboulos' infatuation antedates by far his association with Socrates: this precisely was the reason that Kritoboulos' father handed him over to Socrates to see what he could do about it, and in fact he has already greatly improved although he has kissed Kleinias, and nothing is a greater incitement to passionate desire than a kiss. Socrates disapproves here of kissing youths in their bloom as strongly as he did in his sole conversation with Xenophon that occurs in the Socratic writings; that conversation was also occasioned by Kritoboulos' having kissed a handsome boy; but he does not apostrophize anyone now as he had apostrophized Xenophon then with "you fool" and "you wretch" (*Memorabilia* I.3.8–13), for Xenophon is now invisible and inaudible. Socrates is continent in his speeches (*Memorabilia* I.5.6). Charmides however finds that there is a discrepancy between Socrates' speeches and his deeds; while he scares his friends away from the beautiful youths, Charmides has seen with his own eyes Socrates seeking something with Kritoboulos in the same book in the school, leaning with his head against Kritoboulos' head and with his nude shoulder against Kritoboulos' nude shoulder. (If the harmony between speech and deed is beautiful—cf. Plato, *Laches* 188c6–d8—did Socrates lack beauty also in this respect?) In this way, Xenophon concludes, they mingled pleasantry and seriousness. It is part of the seriousness, I suppose, that Kritoboulos did not prove the superiority of beauty to wisdom.—Antisthenes did not participate in the discussion of Kritoboulos' claim; he was wholly unerotic (cf. 4.38).

Charmides' playful rebuke, not to say accusation, of Socrates, which was not altogether indefensible, gave Kallias—the only one to have hitherto proved the justice of his claim—the occasion to ask Charmides why he was proud of his poverty.

While he was wealthy, he replies, he was always in fear of evils that the others and in particular the city might inflict on him; since he has lost his property, he has no longer any fears but is rather feared by others and is honored by the rich. While he then was a slave, he resembles now a tyrant. While he then paid tribute to the *demos*, he lives now at the expense of the city. While he was rich, he was reproached for being together with Socrates but now no one pays any attention to it. While he was rich, he always lost something through the action of the city or of chance; now he always expects to gain something. (Cf. Montesquieu, *De L'Esprit des lois*, Book VIII, chapter 2.) Kallias asks then whether he wishes to remain poor; Charmides explains that he fearlessly endures the prospect of a change in his condition, the prospect of taking something from somewhere. It seems that he was not willing to remain a partner in the tyranny exercised by the poor citizens for the rest of his life. In the meantime he enjoys his undisturbed association with Socrates. Socrates, who had intervened in all three earlier discussions, is silent about Charmides' speech. He was not the only one among those present to suffer from the tyranny of the Thirty. Under the Thirty, Charmides belonged to the Ten who were in command in the Peiraieus (*Hellenica* II.4.19). It so happens that Kallias and his guests, Xenophon included, and those who stated in chapter 3 of what they are proud are in each case ten. (Cf. also the Ten in Peiraieus in Plato's *Republic*.) Despite the smouldering antagonism which for the time being was only a difference of taste but which was to flare up later into violence and murder, all those present are united by the fact that they are gentlemen. Kritoboulos had been disturbed by the grave conflicts among gentlemen and Socrates had comforted him as only he could (*Memorabilia* II.6.16–27). Kritoboulos' embarrassment points to a hidden am-

biguity of "gentlemanship": Socrates is a gentleman in one
sense of the term while most others are gentlemen in a very
different sense, as Xenophon makes clear in the central chapter
of the *Oeconomicus* by explicitly confronting Socrates' way
of life with that of an outstanding Athenian gentleman. For
such a confrontation the setting of the *Symposium* is most
unsuitable, just as is, if for a different reason, that of the *Memorabilia*, which permits only of a confrontation of Socrates'
way of life with that of a sophist (I.6). Still, the difference
between the two kinds of gentlemanship becomes clear enough
even in the *Symposium* and in the *Memorabilia*.

Charmides, in contradistinction to the first three speakers,
does not claim to make human beings better. He enjoys being
together with Socrates.

Nothing prevents Socrates from asking Antisthenes next
why, having so little, he is proud of his wealth, and thus re-
storing the order which had been disturbed by Charmides, or
by Kallias. He thus contributes to bringing it about that
Antisthenes' speech is the central speech in the chapter. Antisthenes is wealthy in the same sense in which Socrates is
wealthy (*Oeconomicus* II.2–4; cf. *Memorabilia* IV.2.38). In
fact what he says in praise of the kind of wealth that he possesses agrees almost entirely with what Socrates says on other
occasions: he is wealthy because his wants are small; and having
small wants he derives more than sufficient pleasure from satisfying them. He owes his wealth to Socrates, and the most ex-
quisite possession that goes with it, namely, leisure, he uses not
only for seeing what is most worth seeing and hearing what
is most worth hearing but above all for spending all his days
with Socrates in leisure. There are some differences between
his wealth and Socrates', for he lacks the urbanity and delicacy
of his master; he does not see that the praise of frugality and

continence and the blame of lavishness are not quite suitable
to the occasion of a lavish banquet and drinking party. He may
have sensed this somehow since he avoids the term "continence" (*enkrateia*). He also seems to be more willing than
Socrates to converse with all whether they are attractive or
not. (Cf. also 4.40, end, with *Memorabilia* I.3.5, middle.) Kallias responds to Antisthenes' speech with a remark which en-
ables Nikeratos to put his understanding of Homer to what
he thinks is a good use: while Antisthenes has learned from
Socrates' boundless liberality, he has learned from Homer to
count his gifts exactly; he quotes the verses from the *Iliad* in
which Agamemnon enumerated exactly the lavish gifts with
which he was willing to appease Achilleus' wrath; he has
learned from Homer to count, to count money exactly, and
thus perhaps to be rather too fond of money. Thereupon they
all laugh, believing that he had said what is (*ta onta*). This is
the only time in this chapter that anyone is said to have
laughed. (It almost goes without saying that the laughter was
not caused by Philippos.) What is still more remarkable, it is
the only time in the *Symposium* that Socrates laughed. It is
true that Xenophon does not say here explicitly that Socrates
laughed, as he does in the *Apology of Socrates* (28), but Socrates belongs to the "all" who laughed, does he not? Socrates
never laughs in the *Oeconomicus* and in the *Memorabilia*, although he jests there not infrequently, not to say always. Did
he laugh about the suggestion that Homer is a teacher of thrift?
Or did he laugh about the notion that Homer is a teacher of
counting? (Cf. Plato, *Republic* 522d). Or about the notion
that his teaching is diametrically opposed to Homer's? Or did
he laugh about the hidden thought (*hyponoia*) underlying the
counting of a multiple of seven which is the sum of four numbers only one of which ("seven tripods that have not yet been

on fire") is seven? Are the beings numbers? What is perhaps equally remarkable as that all laughed at this point is that none laughs any more in the rest of the *Symposium;* any further laughter would have been anticlimactic. The rest of the work, surely chapters 5–9, is characterized by the greatest seriousness compatible with the circumstances.

The debauch of a general laughter—of the laughter in which Socrates had joined—calls for redress. Someone asks the serious, the very serious Hermogenes to say who the friends are of whom he had spoken and to prove that they have great power and at the same time take care of him; Hermogenes had also spoken of their virtue. He proceeds as follows. All men believe that the gods know everything, both what is and what will be; surely all cities and all tribes practice divination. It is also manifest that we all believe that the gods are able to help and to harm; surely all ask the gods to avert the evil and to bestow the good. Now, these omniscient and omnipotent gods are Hermogenes' friends; because they care for him, neither whither he goes nor what he is about to do is hidden from them. Since they foresee also the outcome, they send him voices, dreams, and birds as messengers and thus indicate what should and what should not be done; if he obeys, he never regrets it but now and then when he did not trust those messengers he was punished. He does not say in so many words that the gods know his silent deliberations or his thoughts but he seems to imply that the gods know his silent deliberations. Socrates, who had been silent about Charmides' and Antisthenes' speeches, now takes the word again: nothing of what Hermogenes had said is incredible but he would be glad to hear by what manner of service he brings it about that the gods are to such an extent his friends. Swearing by Zeus, Hermogenes says that he serves them in a very inexpensive manner; he praises them without spending any money; he always offers part of what they give him; he speaks reverently as much as he can; and when he calls them as witnesses to anything, he does not intentionally say the untruth. He does not explicitly speak of sacrificing. If the poor Socrates was sure not to displease the gods by bringing small sacrifices from his small means, the still poorer Hermogenes did not displease the gods by bringing still smaller sacrifices and perhaps no sacrifices at all (*Memorabilia* I.3.3, II.10). Socrates concludes that if Hermogenes, being a man of the kind that his service to the gods shows him to be, has the gods as friends, the gods too, it seems, take delight in gentlemanship. We note that Socrates did not pretend to be proud of his friendship with the gods; he may have regarded such a claim as boastful or as unsuitable to the occasion. Hermogenes' statement on the inexpensive character of his service to the gods induces us to note that Antisthenes, who was so much concerned with the inexpensive or frugal character of his whole way of life, did not mention his inexpensive service to the gods. The speech of Hermogenes and Socrates, Xenophon concludes, was seriously spoken; the end of this subsection contrasts strikingly with the end of the preceding one.

If at the end of the preceding subsection redress was needed for a superabundance of laughter, now we need some relief from a seriousness which, however appropriate to the subject, would not be altogether suitable in the circumstances. Accordingly Xenophon speaks next of what "they" did when they had come to Philippos; they asked him of course why he was proud of his jesting or more precisely what he saw in jesting to be proud of. The jester is eagerly sought by all, we learn, on joyous occasions, while when some evil befalls them, they run away from him without turning around, since they fear to laugh against their will. According to Nikeratos, Philippos has proved that he is justly proud of his jesting; for to him exactly the reverse happens: when his friends do well, they avoid him but when some evil befalls them, they make every effort to prove to him that they are close relatives of his and never let go of him. Nikeratos, who had caused general laughter in which even Socrates had joined, is indeed the very opposite of a jester. We recall that Socrates was induced to laugh after he had been condemned to die, by a touching manifestation of silliness (*Apology of Socrates* 28).

At this point Charmides, who was perhaps not satisfied with the remedy supplied by the speech of Philippos and Nikeratos' comment on it, again did something quite out of the ordinary. He addressed the Syracusan, who had not been asked in the preceding chapter at all, by asking what he is proud of and whether he is not, as is manifest, proud of the boy. The Syracusan denies this with an oath: he is not proud of him but fears gravely for him because he senses that some are plotting to corrupt (ruin) him. When Socrates heard of "corrupting a young one," he wondered why anyone should wish to kill the boy. The Syracusan is thus forced to explain that the men in question do not wish to kill the boy but to persuade him to sleep with them. Socrates still does not understand: why should the boy thus be corrupted (ruined), especially since the Syracusan sleeps with him the whole night every night; the Syracusan ought to be proud of his flesh since only his flesh does not corrupt those who sleep with him. But the Syracusan is not proud of his flesh; he is proud of the folly of those who look at his puppet shows and thus support him. Philippos confirms that this is the truth. The Syracusan is the only one who does not corrupt the boy by his flesh—this sounds like a ludicrous inversion of Meletos' charge that Socrates is the only one who corrupts the young by his speeches (cf. Plato, *Apology of Socrates* 25a9–11). Is then Socrates proud of his speeches?

Kallias now takes the initiative by addressing the appropriate question to Socrates, who had just discussed with the Syracusan the subject of pederasty. Kallias had once before in this chapter taken the initiative. When Socrates had been jocularly accused by Charmides of being unduly attracted by Kritoboulos' youthful bloom, he had asked Charmides to justify his being proud of his poverty. Now he asks Socrates to justify his being proud of the disreputable art of procuring. He and the others bypass Lykon and Autolykos, who are proud of things which are not in need of, or not susceptible of, justifying speeches. It thus comes about that Socrates takes the place at the end—the place which in the preceding chapter had been occupied by Hermogenes: Socrates and Hermogenes are in a manner interchangeable; both are, if in different ways, outstandingly pious. Socrates proposes that in the first place they reach agreement as to the work of the good procurer, just as he tried in the case of controversy to establish in the first place agreement as to the work of the good citizen (*Memorabilia* IV.6.14); he will ask questions and the others should answer. " 'Do you agree to that?' he said. 'Certainly,' they said. Once they had said 'Certainly,' they all gave this reply from then on." No hitch occurred while Socrates asked whether the good procurer must not render pleasing her or him whom he prostitutes, to those with whom she or he is to be together; whether in order to be pleasing they must not among other things have a becoming arrangement of hair and of dress; whether the good procurer must not teach those whom he offers how to look affectionately, how to speak with a modest voice, and how to say things that lead to friendship, in a word, whether he must not teach

them how to look and to speak pleasantly. To all these questions they all replied "Certainly." They all said "Certainly"
altogether seven times. But then Socrates raised a question to
which no single or simple answer, it seems, can be given. He
asked who is the better procurer—he who is able to render his
clients pleasing to one or he who can render them pleasing also
to many. At this point they split, some saying, "He who renders him pleasing to most," the others saying, "Certainly." The
latter obviously did not wish to state the unpopular alternative.
But Socrates, who had taken as his model the safe speaker
Odysseus and could more than anybody else Xenophon knew
present his hearers as agreeing (*Memorabilia* IV.6.15), presented them as agreeing by saying that they were in agreement
also on this point (or by burying the opposition through silence) and continued: would not he who renders his clients
pleasing to the whole city be the altogether perfect procurer?
Thereupon all replied, "Manifestly, by Zeus." The unpopular
alternative is then that the individual, or the individual of a
certain kind, is to be preferred to the whole city. It will come
to the fore before long. Socrates draws the final conclusion,
while ceasing to speak of the procurer and speaking instead of
him who presides: if he can do what was previously called the
work of the altogether perfect procurer, he would justly be
proud of his art and justly receive ample pay. To this too they
all agreed. Socrates had said that he was proud of his art of
procuring. But now after he has proved beyond any shadow
of doubt that that art deserves to be proud of, he declares
that Antisthenes is the altogether perfect procurer. Antisthenes
understands this to mean that Socrates hands over to him the
art of which he is proud. One wonders whether Antisthenes
thus became good at teaching people to look pleasingly and
to speak pleasingly. But Socrates seems to have no qualms,

for according to him Antisthenes has also perfect command of the art accompanying the art of the procurer, namely, the art of the pimp or the go-between. Antisthenes was naturally greatly angered by this praise but Socrates appeased him quickly by showing him that what he had in mind is a highly laudatory practice: Antisthenes acted as a go-between between, and brought together, Kallias and the wise Prodikos as well as Hippias of Elis; he inflamed Socrates with a passionate desire for, and then brought him together with, the stranger from Heraklea and Aischylos the Phleiousian; a man who can bring together individuals who are useful to one another and make them desire one another can establish friendship among cities, arrange fitting marriages, and the like. The men with whom Antisthenes brought Kallias or Socrates together were all strangers, i.e., not parts of the city. Socrates, who could act as a procurer to the city but does not wish to exercise that art, hands it over to Antisthenes, who is eager to accept it. Socrates would rather remain the beneficiary of Antisthenes' "pimping," which brings him together with individuals who interest him keenly because he can learn from them. The question which is left open in the *Memorabilia* (I.2.48 and 6.15) is answered in the *Symposium.*

Chapter 5

Only Kallias, Nikeratos, and Socrates were proud of an art. But Nikeratos could not show that the knowledge which he possesses is an art. Only Kallias and Socrates have shown that they are justly proud of their art. Thus the stage is set for a contest on wisdom between Kallias and Socrates. But Xenophon forgoes this possibility. Instead he makes Kallias ask Kritoboulos to enter the lists in the beauty contest with Socrates. Kritoboulos is not afraid: Socrates will have to show that he is more beautiful than Kritoboulos but both contestants must be clearly visible; Socrates' speech will have to be examined in the light of the lamp. Socrates addresses questions to Kritoboulos in his usual manner but this time the questioning is forensic (cf. *Education of Cyrus* III.1.6–13); it does not concern the "what is" of beauty but the beauty of the two contestants. It is true that one cannot decide the forensic question without having settled first the philosophic question. But this does not cause any difficulty: Kritoboulos knows—he has learned from Socrates on other occasions—that things are beautiful if they are well-adapted by art or nature with a view to our actions or to our needs. As Socrates had put it to Aristippos: human bodies as well as everything else are called both beautiful and good in the same respect, namely, in relation to the things for which they can be well used (*Memorabilia* III.8.5). Socrates is now going to apply this understanding of the beauty of human bodies to his and Kritoboulos' body. He proves with ease that his bulging eyes and his snubbed nose together with his wide nostrils are more beautiful than Kritoboulos' eyes and nose since they are more useful for seeing and smelling. (Since the parts of the body have been given to us by the gods it appears that Socrates has been treated by the gods in regard to his body too better than other men; cf. *Memorabilia* IV.3.12). Thereupon Kritoboulos grants spontaneously that if the mouth has been made for the purpose of biting off, Socrates has a more beautiful mouth than he, and his thick lips are better adapted to kissing softly than his. Socrates is aware that in Kritoboulos' view his mouth is uglier than that of an ass; he reminds him therefore of the fact that the Naiads, being goddesses, give birth to Silenuses who resemble him more than they resemble Kritoboulos. If Socrates is as ugly as a Silenus, he has at least a mother of divine beauty (Phainarete). Then at Kritoboulos' demand a secret vote is

taken; all gave the prize to Kritoboulos. This proves to Socrates that Kritoboulos' money seems to differ from Kallias' in
that Kallias' money makes people more just while Kritoboulos',
like most other money, has rather the opposite effect. The
beauty contest proves in fact that Socrates is ugly also in this
respect, that his simple equation of the beautiful with the useful is untrue. Taken literally, it leads to a crude, calculating
utilitarianism for which friends are pieces of property (*Memorabilia* II.4–5 and 10; cf. III.4; *Oeconomicus* I.14). The
beautiful (noble) cannot be reduced to the good (useful) in
the first place because the city and its interests cannot be reduced to the self-interest of the individuals: what is good for
the city, is frequently noble rather than good for the individual
(*Memorabilia* III.5.28; cf. I.1.8 and III.1.1); and in the second
place because the beautiful in a different sense is good for the
beholder rather than for the user (*Memorabilia* II.2.3). There
is a connection between these two very different reasons and
the two alternatives adumbrated at the end of the preceding
chapter. Socrates loses the contest concerning *kallos* (beauty,
nobility) because he has repudiated the most noble virtue and
greatest art, the kingly art (*Memorabilia* IV.2.11). Immediately
afterward he will be refuted by Hermogenes.

The *Symposium* is the only Socratic writing of Xenophon in
which Socrates' body (or a part of it) is described, just as it
is the only one of these writings in which his marriage is discussed. These "comic" subjects are not brought up by the
professional jester Philippos: the poor parasite cannot afford
to bring them up; he surely is unable to see the serious things
of which they are the comical equivalents.

Chapter 6

There followed two disturbances, one caused by Hermogenes, the other caused by the Syracusan. Kritoboulos' victory

was celebrated with some pleasantries in which all shared with the exception of Hermogenes, who even then remained silent. Socrates tried to induce him to be somewhat more pleasing to the company by addressing to him an appropriate "what is" question: Xenophon underlines the fact that Socrates called him by name (cf. Plato, *Cratylus*); Hermogenes cannot answer that question but can only say what "it seems"; this is sufficient for Socrates' present purpose. The exchange leads to the result that Socrates is refuted by Hermogenes and calls Kallias to come to his help. Kallias makes a suggestion which Socrates slightly modifies: Hermogenes should speak in the future to the accompaniment of the flute; thus his speeches will become somewhat sweetened. Kallias then wonders what would be the proper musical accompaniment when Antisthenes will refute someone at the banquet. Antisthenes makes a suggestion which is not very graceful. The "refuters" Hermogenes and Antisthenes are in different ways in need of sweetening or of grace.

While such speeches were made, the Syracusan saw that the company did not pay attention to his show but were enjoying one another and thus he became envious of Socrates. He said: Are you, Socrates, the one who is nicknamed the thinker (worrier), because you are thought to be a thinker of the things aloft? Socrates countered this allusion to his alleged impiety by asking the Syracusan whether he knows anything more aloft than the gods. But, the Syracusan continues his attack: according to what people say, Socrates cares, not for the gods, but about the most useless things. Socrates shows with the help of a pun that even so he would care about the gods (there are gods who are not the gods of the city): "If I speak frigidly, it is your fault since you cause me troubles." The Syracusan does not let go of Socrates: he refers to Socrates' peculiar "geometry" which measures a flea's jump in terms of a flea's feet. Before Socrates can reply Antisthenes intervenes; he asks Philippos to liken the Syracusan to someone or something, for he resembles someone wishing to scold. Antisthenes calls on the jester to defend Socrates against attacks borrowed from Aristophanes; Philippos is only too willing to do it; Philippos' taking Socrates' side is a comic equivalent of the true relation between Aristophanes and Socrates. But Socrates forbids Philippos to say anything about the Syracusan, for anything he would say about him would in the circumstances resemble abuse: Socrates does not need anybody's help for appeasing the Syracusan, whereas he needed Kallias' help against Hermogenes.

Hermogenes' refutation of Socrates and the Syracusan's attack on Socrates belong together. For the time being nothing worse happens than a minor annoyance. Still, that annoyance forebodes Socrates' condemnation, just as the Syracusan's envy of Socrates forebodes the Athenians' or the fathers' envy of him. Just as Charmides' presence and speech foreshadow the sanguinary rule of the Thirty, Socrates' violent death is foreshadowed by the presence of Lykon, one of Socrates' three accusers, whose son was so proud of his father that he was in no danger of being corrupted by Socrates.

Chapter 7

Socrates succeeds easily in winning over the Syracusan while, or by, finding fault with his show; by teaching him what he ought to do in order to achieve his end, he seems to take him seriously. He grants him that he indeed runs the risk of being, as the Syracusan says, a thinker; therefore he wonders whether the Syracusan's aim—to please the spectators—is achieved by the performances which he proposes, namely, a

dangerous sword dance and other farfetched wonders: if someone wants to look at wonders, he has only to wonder at what is
right at hand; for instance why the lamp, because it has a
bright flame, gives light, whereas the bronze body of the lamp,
although it is also bright, does not give light but shows within
itself other things mirrored; and how oil, being liquid, nour-
ishes the flame, while water, owing to its being liquid, extin-
guishes fire. But these things too, just like the shows which the
Syracusan was preparing, go ill together with a drinking party.
Socrates does not say that these "physiological" questions are
not serious or beyond man's reach but that they are too serious
for a drinking party. Still, he who never speaks of this kind of
question in the other Socratic writings of Xenophon, speaks
of them in an advanced stage of a drinking party where a
greater *parrhesia* is in order than elsewhere: the "physiological" part of his wisdom, nay, his whole wisdom can be
shown without disguise only "in fun"; so close is the connection between wisdom and laughter. Yet even at that drinking
party at which some refuters or attackers are present, Socrates
exercises some restraint; he speaks only of a physiologist's question regarding terrestrial things as distinguished from heavenly
or divine ones (*Memorabilia* I.1.11–13, IV.7.4–7). Socrates proposes to the Syracusan that his boy and the girl should present
to the accompaniment of the flute dance figures of the Graces,
the Horai, and the Nymphs; the Syracusan is eager to oblige.

Chapter 8

When the Syracusan left in order to prepare a graceful
show, Socrates started another speech. Eros, a mighty daimon,
being present, they should all remember him, especially since
they all are votaries of that god. They all—Socrates, Charmides, Kritoboulos, Nikeratos, and Hermogenes—are lovers,

although not all of them lovers of human beings; Hermogenes is in love with perfect gentlemanship, whatever it may be, as was shown by his whole demeanor, with which we have been made thoroughly familiar through the *Symposium;* Hermogenes' love is surely connected with his enjoying the friendship of the most august gods (cf. 4.49). Socrates asks Antisthenes whether he alone is not in love with someone. He replies that he is passionately in love with Socrates. Socrates in mock coyness urges him not to cause him any trouble at present since, as he sees, he is occupied with other things. But Antisthenes says that Socrates, this "procurer" of himself, never has time for Antisthenes' love; sometimes he uses the *daimonion* as pretext (he apparently does not believe in the truthfulness of the *daimonion*—cf. *Memorabilia* I.1.4–5 and Plato, *Apology of Socrates* 37e5 ff.) and sometimes he longs for someone or something else (cf. *Memorabilia* III.11.16–18); in both ways he avoids conversing with him. Socrates implores Antisthenes to desist from his attack on him; otherwise he bears and will bear with his harshness or ill-temper in a spirit of friendship, but his *eros* should be concealed; especially since it is directed not toward Socrates' soul but toward his visible beauty. This is another jocular expression for what he had expressed jocularly before by handing over his art of procuring to Antisthenes (4.60–61). Socrates speaks next of Kallias as a lover. He thus has shown that all gentlemen present are lovers; he has naturally omitted Lykon, who cares only for his beautiful son. But we must not forget the invisible and inaudible Xenophon, for he too is a lover, in fact he is as much as his Antisthenes a lover of Socrates, but distinguished from the harsh and pedantic Antisthenes by his light-heartedness, grace, and flexibility. It is difficult to believe that his love was not requited.

The rest of Socrates' long speech on Eros, i.e., its bulk, is addressed to Kallias. For its proper understanding one must remember that Kallias was in love not only with Autolykos but also with philosophy (4.62; cf. 1.4), just as the Platonic Socrates was in love with Alkibiades, the son of Kleinias, and philosophy (*Gorgias* 481d1–5). Socrates will be completely silent henceforth on Kallias' love for philosophy and in fact on philosophy altogether. His speech will be altogether political, and if it transcends the political, it transcends it not toward philosophy but toward the mythical.

If we can trust Socrates, he has always admired Kallias' nature but now that Kallias loves Autolykos, he admires him still more, for his beloved exhibits to all strength as well as endurance, manliness, and moderation. Socrates does not know whether there is only one Aphrodite or two—the Heavenly and the Vulgar—but he does know that the cults of the two differ. One might conjecture that Vulgar Aphrodite sends love of the bodies, while the Heavenly sends love of the souls as well as of friendship and of noble deeds. If, as Socrates does not exclude, there is only one Aphrodite, both kinds of *eros* have one and the same source and a simple opposition of them is not possible. Kallias, as it seems to Socrates, is possessed by the heavenly *eros*, as is shown in particular by the fact that he is together with Autolykos only in the presence of his beloved's father. At this point there occurs an interruption —the only interruption of Socrates' speech in praise of Eros or of Kallias. Hermogenes must say that he admires Socrates in many other respects but also for his now at the same time gratifying Kallias and educating him in what kind of man he ought to be. His deplorable heavy-handedness (consider the contrast with *Memorabilia* III.524)—his complete lack of understanding of what irony is or requires—confirms everything that the *Symposium* had suggested regarding him before. Socrates of course makes the best use of his interruption: in order to please Kallias still more, he wishes to bear witness to him that the *eros* of the soul is much more excellent than the *eros* of the body. As we all know, there is no being together worth mentioning without friendship. Friendship on the part of those who admire someone on account of his character is called a pleasant and voluntary necessity, while many of those who desire the body, blame and hate the ways of their beloved. It is possible no doubt to be fond of someone on account of both his character and the beauty of his body but when the youthful bloom begins to decay, friendship would perish with it, were there not also fondness on account of character. In the enjoyment of the body there is surfeit, which is much less the case in friendship of the souls, for in spite of its purity it is not deprived of Aphrodite's graces. Socrates seems to hesitate between the praise of a love that is directed only to the soul of the beloved and the praise of a love that is directed also to his beautiful body (cf. 4.27). This cannot be explained sufficiently by his ignorance as to whether there is only one Aphrodite or whether the Heavenly Aphrodite is a being different from the Vulgar one, for this ignorance is itself in need of explanation. The explanation is that Socrates praises *eros* "with a view to" Kallias, who is in love with the beautiful youth Autolykos. He goes on to show that the noble lover is likely to be loved in turn by his beloved and that their friendship may well last till their old age. (The thought that it may last till the old age of both is naturally absent from the parallel in *Hiero* 3.) But on the other hand the youth who is loved only on account of his body is only repelled by his lover. To mention only one of Socrates' arguments, a youth and a man do not share the pleasures in the sexual act, as a man and a woman do, but the sober youth looks on the man who is drunk with sexual desire. We venture to draw this conclusion, which is subject to the qualification touched upon shortly before: love (*eros*) of the soul alone is necessarily love of a male human being for another; if love of the body is joined to love of the soul, man's love of woman is by far superior to his homosexual love. The heavenly *eros* which strives for lasting friendship between lover and beloved makes both lover and beloved concerned with the exercise of virtue, especially of continence and sense of shame. As a matter of fact, the greatest good for him who desires to make his beloved a good friend is that he himself must exercise virtue. Socrates shows then through selected myths that gods and heroes too esteem the friendship of the soul more highly than the enjoyment of the body. All mortal women whom Zeus loved and with whom he had intercourse on account of their bodily beauty were left by him in their mortal state while he made immortal those whom he admired and with whom he had intercourse on account of the goodness of their souls. But Zeus loved of course not only women but also Ganymedes; regarding him, Socrates affirms that Zeus had carried him up to Olympos on account, not of his body, but of his soul. When speaking of the heroes or half-gods, Socrates mentions only their relations to their male friends—relations free from bodily desire and inspired only by mutual admiration which led to joint action of the greatest grandeur and nobility. Socrates turns then to the noble deeds performed in the present time; they too are the work of those who are willing to toil and to run dangers for the sake of praise rather than of those who are in the habit of choosing pleasure in preference to noble fame. In spite of this Pausanias, the lover of the poet Agathon, speaking in defense of the dissolute has said that an army composed of beloved and lovers would be of outstanding bravery; he supported this sentiment by a specious reasoning and by the testimony of the Thebans and the Eleans, among whom according to him the lovers and beloved sleep together and are comrades in arms. Socrates rejects this example as irrelevant: the Thebans and Eleans regard sleeping together of lover and beloved as lawful while to "us" (Athenians) it is disgraceful. He knows of course that this counterargument is irrelevant as regards the compatibility, so vehemently denied by him, of dissoluteness and bravery, just as he knows that a man may be an adulterer and yet be fit to rule (cf. *Memorabilia* II.1.5); the superiority of love of the soul to love of the body cannot be established on the plane of manliness and even of political life as a whole. But whatever the Thebans and Eleans may approve of, the Spartans are in full agreement with the Athenians, and the confirmation by Sparta, the hegemonial city par excellence, is obviously decisive. Furthermore, even the votary of vulgar love would have a greater trust in a boy who is lovable in respect of his soul than in a boy whom he loves because of the beauty of his body.

Socrates then turns to Kallias again. He must be grateful that the gods have inspired him with love for such an excellent youth as Autolykos, who might well come to believe that he will be able to adorn not only himself and his father but his fatherland by gaining victories over her enemies and that he would thus become celebrated among both Greeks and barbarians: would he not honor with the greatest honors him whom he would regard as his most excellent fellow worker in this pursuit? But in order to please Autolykos, Kallias would have to consider what things Themistokles understood in order to become able to liberate Greece; he would have to consider what things Perikles knew so that he seemed to be a most excellent counselor to the fatherland; he would have to observe in what manner Solon had philosophized before he laid down

most excellent laws to the city; and he would have to inquire
by the practice of what kind of things the Spartans seem to be
most excellent leaders—the Spartans who are Kallias' guest-
friends and the most excellent among whom always stay with
him when they are in Athens. After he has acquired all this
knowledge, the city would eagerly entrust itself to him, provided he wishes it, for he is a patrician, a priest of the divinities
of Eleusis, and in exercising his priestly functions he has an
even more impressive appearance than his predecessors, as he
possesses a body most becoming to behold and sturdy. Then
addressing the company Socrates apologizes if they think that
he has spoken with greater seriousness than is suitable to a
drinking party; but he always is and remains a fellow lover
together with the city of those who are good by nature and
long for virtue ambitiously: he does not count Kallias among
those who possess good natures in the precise sense (*Memorabilia* IV.1.2) or who have a soul by nature good (*Oeconomicus* XI.5–6). Kallias, with half an eye to Autolykos, asked
Socrates whether he, the avowed procurer, will prostitute him
to the city, so that he will take care of its affairs and be always
pleasing to his city. Socrates does this indeed but Kallias must
be earnestly concerned with virtue and no god must hinder.

Socrates' long speech on *eros*, nay, his whole action in the
Symposium, culminates in his acting as a matchmaker between
Kallias and the city. From what we observed regarding the
inferiority of love of women to love of the souls of men, he
could not well have acted as a matchmaker between Kallias and
a woman and in particular the daughter of Ischomachos, the
hero of the *Oeconomicus*. Socrates exercises the art of the altogether excellent matchmaker as it were for the last time, after
he had already abandoned it to Antisthenes. While Antisthenes
had acted as a matchmaker between Kallias and Prodikos as

well as Hippias (IV.62), Socrates acts as a matchmaker between Kallias and the city. He exercises this art now "in fun."
This is precisely his deed performed in fun which is his only
deed to speak of, for deeds lack the seriousness of speeches (cf.
Plato, *Apology of Socrates* 32a5 and *Republic* 473a1–4). Or,
what is apparently more precise, he exercises his art in fun
when acting as a matchmaker between the city and Kallias,
while he exercises it in seriousness when acting as a matchmaker between the city and Charmides (*Memorabilia* III.7).
Through the presentation of Charmides in the *Symposium*,
Xenophon justifies abundantly his disregard of that serious
deed of Socrates. As for Kallias, Socrates tries to free him
from his hopeless *eros* for philosophy and to instill him with an
eros for an outstanding career as a statesman. How successful
Kallias (and therefore Socrates) was, can be seen from the
Hellenica (VI.3).

Chapter 9

After the brief exchange between Socrates and Kallias that
followed Socrates' long speech, we hear no further word from
Socrates. Autolykos left the dining hall in order to take an
exercise. His father, Lykon, going out with him, turned around
and said: "By Hera, Socrates, you seem to me to be a human
being who is noble and good." He did not call Socrates "a
man who is noble and good," "a perfect gentleman." He thus
expresses the same thought which Xenophon expresses by failing to count manliness among Socrates' virtues. However
pachydermic he was, somehow he had sensed that Socrates was
not a perfect gentleman in the sense in which he understood
that expression.

Then the Syracusan presented his show, a pantomime of
Ariadne's and Dionysos' love, played by the dancing girl and

the boy. Ariadne was dressed as a bride; Dionysos had drunk a bit together with gods. While the play progressed, the boy and the girl ceased to pretend to kiss one another but kissed one another truly with their lips; they obviously were deeply in love; the play gave them the permission to do what they had desired to do for long. When the spectators saw them in each other's arms and about to go to the couch, the unmarried among them swore that they would marry; but those who were married jumped on their horses and rode off to enjoy their wives; Socrates however and the others who stayed, i.e., the unmarried, went out with Kallias to join Lykon and his son in their walk.

The work of the Syracusan consists in bringing together men and women or rather husbands and wives; he is in no sense a procurer. The work of Socrates consists in bringing together men good by nature and the city. But while the Syracusan exercises his trade without any irony, the same cannot be said of Socrates' pandering. Socrates had a certain influence on the Syracusan; while he did not do what Socrates had advised him to do, he ceased doing things of which Socrates explicitly disapproved. The Syracusan had no influence on Socrates: while the Syracusan's final exhibition incited or excited "the married ones" to hurry home to enjoy their wives, the married Socrates stayed behind; he behaved like an inveterate bachelor. His relation to Xanthippe is the comic equivalent of his relation to the city.

As for Xenophon's choice of a Syracusan as the antagonist of Socrates, I fear that its explanation may depend on the explanation of "Themistogenes of Syracuse," the author of a book which is indistinguishable from Xenophon's *Anabasis* (*Hellenica* III.1.2).

⚂⚂⚂⚂⚂ Appendix

The now prevailing view of Xenophon which its holders are likely to consider as balanced or moderate presupposes an extreme or reckless questioning of him as a classic, as a man to look up to, as an authority. The most telling testimony of such questioning is the judgment of B. G. Niebuhr: "Truly no state has ever expelled a more degenerate son than this Xenophon. Plato too was not a good citizen; he was not worthy of Athens, he has taken incomprehensible steps, he stands like a sinner against the saints, Thucydides and Demosthenes, but yet how altogether differently from this old fool!" ("Über Xenophon's Hellenika," *Kleine historische und philosophische Schriften*, I [Bonn, 1828], 467). Niebuhr was a great Prussian patriot; he participated most nobly in the resistance to Napoleon and in the politics of the Restoration; he was a great admirer of Burke. He was a patriot who was insufficiently aware of the fact that "patriotism is not enough" and hence that there are times and circumstances in which it is more noble to desert to the enemy and to fight against one's fatherland than to do what is ordinarily most noble. Aristotle has indicated the premise from which one must start in order to find some light in this thicket by reminding us of two views of the good citizen; according to one view, "good citizen" is relative to the regime while according to the other the good citizen is a man who serves his city well under any regime (*Politics* 1276b30–31; *Resp. Ath.* 28.5).

The abstraction from the difference of regimes is sanctioned by the word "fatherland." I propose to discuss the use of "fatherland" (*patris*) in Xenophon's Socratic writings.

In the *Memorabilia, patris* occurs for the first time in II.1, in Socrates' conversation with Aristippos, who leads, and wishes to lead, the life of a stranger; immediately after Aristippos has expressed this view, Socrates uses *patris*, clearly not with the intention to appeal to nonexistent lofty sentiments; he uses the word again in the general exhortation with which he concludes his argument and shortly before he turns to his rendering of Prodikos' story of Herakles at the crossroads. In that story, Virtue speaks of *patris* when speaking to Heracles, who is not (yet) her friend, about her friends; when she speaks to Heracles about him, she does not speak of *patris* but of "some city": Heracles is free to choose any city; he does not have a fatherland, since his father is Zeus (II.1.14, 19, 33; cf. II.1.28).

Patris occurs next in II.6.25, in Socrates' speech to Kritoboulos; then in III.5.3, in Socrates' speech to Perikles; then in III.6.2, in Socrates' speech to Glaukon; then in III.7.1, in Socrates' speech to Charmides. Hitherto *patris* occurred only in political (not merely military or private) contexts and it occurred in all emphatically political contexts. From this we understand Socrates' using *patris* in III.12.4 to signify that his conversation with Epigenes is emphatically political—the only political conversation in III.8–14. Socrates speaks of *patris* thereafter only in IV.2.33 (to Euthydemos) and in IV.4.14 (to Hippias). I refer to my comment on IV.4.14.

In the *Oeconomicus*, *patris* occurs only in IV.3, in a Socratic exhortation to Kritoboulos (cf. *Memorabilia* II.6.25).

In the *Symposium* Charmides speaks of the *patris* when he justifies his being proud on account of his poverty (4.29), and Socrates in his long speech when exhorting Autolykos on the one hand and Kallias on the other (8.38 and 39). Charmides is the only character other than Socrates who speaks of *patris* in the Socratic writings. For the interpretation of what he says, see my *On Tyranny* (Ithaca, N.Y.: Cornell University Press), p. 58.

The most important Xenophontic statement on the fatherland—*Anabasis* III.1.4—cannot be properly interpreted except within the context of an interpretation of the *Anabasis* as a whole.

ꙮꙮꙮꙮ Index